T0064803

All's Fair in Love & Wardrobe

All's Fair in Love & Wardrobe

A Fashion Editor's Rules on Shopping for Love

Stephanie Simons
Illustrations by Malia Carter

Skyhorse Publishing

Copyright © 2014 by Stephanie Simons
Illustration copyright © 2014 by Malia Carter

All Rights Reserved. No part of this book may be reproduced in any manner without the express written consent of the publisher, except in the case of brief excerpts in critical reviews or articles. All inquiries should be addressed to Skyhorse Publishing, 307 West 36th Street, 11th Floor, New York, NY 10018.

Skyhorse Publishing books may be purchased in bulk at special discounts for sales promotion, corporate gifts, fund-raising, or educational purposes. Special editions can also be created to specifications. For details, contact the Special Sales Department, Skyhorse Publishing, 307 West 36th Street, 11th Floor, New York, NY 10018 or info@skyhorsepublishing.com.

Skyhorse® and Skyhorse Publishing® are registered trademarks of Skyhorse Publishing, Inc.®, a Delaware corporation.

www.skyhorsepublishing.com

10 9 8 7 6 5 4 3 2 1

Library of Congress Cataloging-in-Publication Data is available on file.

Cover illustration by: Malia Carter

ISBN: 978-1-62914-296-8
EISBN: 978-1-62914-322-4

Printed in China

To all the girls who've ever wanted
to shop, dress, eat, party, travel,
and Instagram like a fashion editor.
Now you can date like one.

*Fashion editors have the best dating stories. The late nights. The
champagne hangovers. The bold-faced names. If only the accessories closet
at *Vogue* could talk . . .

ELLE

412+
BEST
PIECES

KATE
HUDSON

HOW TO
LOSE A GUY
IN 10 SECONDS

HOW TO FIND THE
PROBLEM AND
FIX IT

How to date like a fashion editrix, a crash course

Kiss on the *chic*

At the end of the night, when your date goes in for an unwanted lip lock, call him *dahling*, turn a glowing cheek, and air kiss with the elegance and minty fresh breath of Grace Coddington canoodling with the boys of Proenza Schouler backstage at a show. *"Mwah! Mwah! Thank you for a lovely time!"* Crisis averted.

Become an acronympho

Acronyms like *OTK* (over-the-knee) and *VPL* (visible panty line) are linguistic Morse code used by fashion editors in order to purposely confuse the rest of the world. Speaking like this in real life with your single girlfriends will allow you to talk about a leering creeper right in front of him, without him even realizing it. *OMG! PSM! WSG! ("Oh my gah! Please save me! Weird staring guy!")*

Have a long lead time

Thursday is the new Wednesday when it comes to securing plans. If he's totally interested in you, expect him to stake his claim on your Saturday night by Thursday evening. If he's texting you an invitation to tag along at the last minute, without allowing enough time to shave your legs or change your outfit, it's probably because someone else canceled on him.

Channel a front-row state of mind

Being in love's "front row" means securing prime seating alongside his best friends and eventually earning a backstage pass to hang with his family. Don't settle for being the back-row babe who's constantly shuffled around and buried out of sight under the proverbial exit sign.

Worship at the altar of *The Comma Sutra*

You can tell a lot about a man by his punctuation and prose via email and text. Regarding vocabulary, size matters. Also pay close attention to his response time (*two seconds versus two days*), word choice (*you versus ya*), and berserk use of emoticons.

Don't rush to meet deadlines

Slow and steady wins the race when it comes to making romantic decisions involving the rest of your life, but there may come a time when you reach a certain age and everyone starts getting married and having kids like it's going out of style. If friends and family try to pressure you, tell them recent advances in anticellulite jeans and tush-toning sneakers promise to extend your prime while you take your sweet time.

Move on with style

A fashion editor doesn't cling to the memory of her former boyfriend jeans when they're kaput. Instead, she swiftly moves on to the next big thing, which she's already had her eye on for the last couple of seasons. Let this forward-thinking mantra guide you after a break-up and above all, remember: When God closes a door, he opens a Neiman Marcus.

Know what makes a great cover story

And by great cover story, we mean brilliant exit strategy. The cell phone is a cruel little invention that's made it virtually impossible to give an overly amorous aggressor *faux* digits. That's because once you give it to him, he's likely to dial you up as he stands next to you (this is his way of programming his number into your phone, and making sure it actually rings). The phantom boyfriend excuse still works in a pinch, but since it could backfire in the presence of other attractive men, we suggest slipping unwanted suitors your new email address EditrixMinx@gmail.com. We'll have our unpaid interns take care of his correspondence the same way they take care of our endless PR spam.

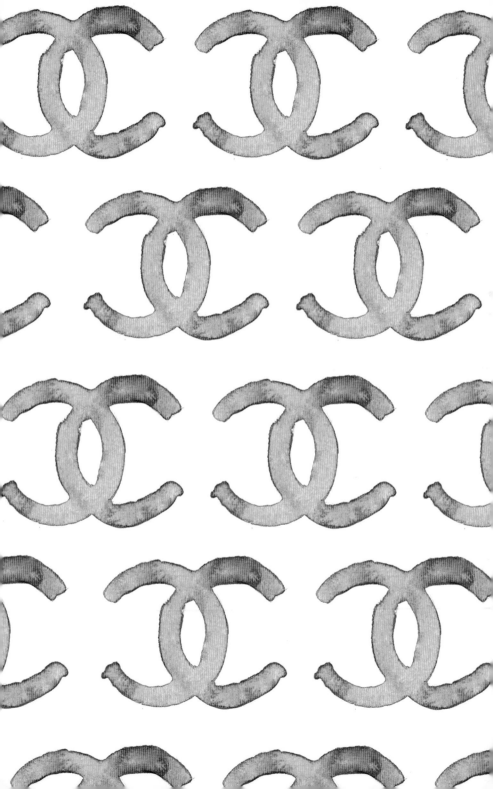

Rule 1

When in doubt, date like an editrix.

It's all about mastering the art of the edit. ~~Buy less, choose well.~~ Date less, choose well. Being more selective about the men you spend time with will inevitably save you a lot of grief in the long run. Alas, without the "worst date ever" horror stories in your back pocket you'll have to find another way to be the highlight of every cocktail party. (May we suggest a crystal-beaded sheath?)

Rule 2

Men ask for numbers they'll never call, like women buy clothes they'll never wear.

Don't take it personally. If anyone knows how it feels to be smitten by an irresistible sequin mini in the moment but never drum up the courage to take it out on the town, it's you. Why men say what they don't mean (especially when they don't have to) is one of life's greatest mind-bogglers, right up there with mullet skirts and jeggings. It is what it is, and it happens to everyone. Never let it bring you down, gorgeous.

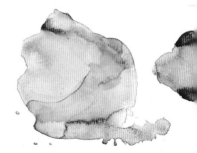

The 7 phases of waiting for him to call

Phase 1 (day 1)

"I just met the greatest guy ever! I can't wait to go out with him!"

Phase 2 (day 2)

"Oh, hi Mom. No, I thought you were someone else calling. Can you stop doing that for the next 48–72 hours, please?"

Phase 3 (day 3)

"Are you kidding me? Guys still play by the three day rule?" *<eye roll>*

Phase 4 (day 4)

"What if my business card got washed to shreds in his pants pocket? Should I just go for it and call him?" *<consults Magic Eight Ball>*

Phase 5 (day 5)

"Hello, Verizon Wireless? Can you confirm my phone is fully functioning?"

Phase 6 (day 6)

"Well, even if he does call, I'm not picking up." *<high five to self>*

Phase 7 (day 7)

"Oh well, he wasn't my type anyway. Next!"

Rule 3

Believe in love at first sight, beyond the window display at
your favorite jewelry boutique.

It's that twinkling, hypnotic, know-it-when-you-see-it, can't-live-
without-it quality that makes everything else dull by comparison.
And it can strike anywhere. Never lose sight of all the glamorous,
goose-bumpy possibilities.

Rule 4

At some point a man may informally say to you,
"Let's get married!" Without jewelry as collateral, this is
merely his way of putting your love on layaway.

Ring pops, Mardi Gras beads, and edible party favors do
not count as jewelry.

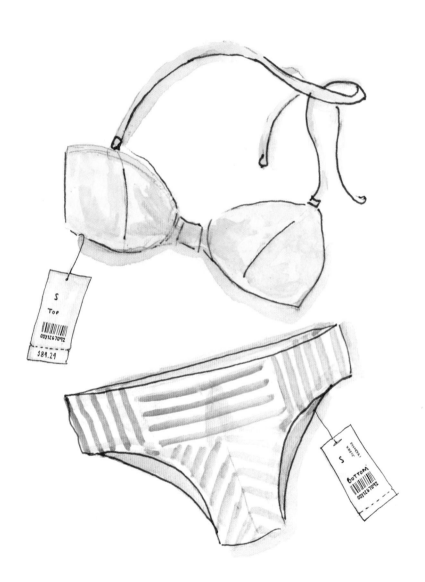

Rule 5

Unlike the tags on that bikini you wish you could take back, you don't need to be attached.

Needing a romantic attachment and wanting one are two entirely separate things. A man is by no means a must-have.

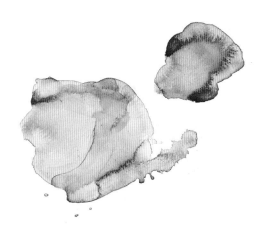

Rule 6

Master the art of color blocking.

Rock a shocking combination of colors so bright that you prevent other women in the room from being noticed. Next to having a C-note or piece of Beef Jerky sticking out of your pocket, wearing brights remains the best way to get a guy to sit up and take notice of you. The more electric the hue, the more electricity you'll create.

Rule 7

It's okay if you'd rather stay home on Friday night, wearing your faithful Juicy pants and watching your toenail polish dry.

Even Jennifer Lawrence, Hollywood's hottest leading lady, admits there are times when she'd rather be at home watching reality television than hobnobbing with suits. Sometimes it's more fun to kickback on the couch with a paper plate full of Bagel Bites than it is to sit through a fancy six-course dinner with a guy who wants to riddle you with questions like, *"So tell me about yourself? Who are you? Where do you see yourself in five years? What's your full life story, from beginning to end?"*

clothes
before
bros

Rule 8

~~Bros before hos.~~

Wear whatever makes you stand tall, even if it makes you taller than him, and wear whatever makes you feel pretty, even if it makes you more overdressed than him. The more you style yourself to please men, the more naked and degenerate-looking you will eventually become. See also: "support hose before bros," the golden rule for single women entering their twilight years.

TRENDS WITH BENEFITS

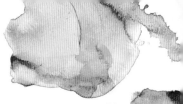

Since the beginning of time, fashion and passion have been inextricably linked, from the first fig leaf worn in the Garden of Eden to the venerable wedding gown. Every now and then, a modern fashion designer's influence still leaves an indelible mark on courtship. Herewith, a few important dates in the history of dating:

4000 BC The first lingerie, inspired by fig leaves, is designed by original sinners Adam and Eve.

1500 A .07 waist-to-hip ratio, the most feminine of wiles, is made possible by the waist-cinching corset.

1700 Rise of the scarf. Perfect for hiding love bites around the neck in a time of staunch conservatism.

1800 The turtleneck trumps the scarf as a means of hiding one's saggy neck from younger suitors.

1850 With the zipper comes unprecedented ease in undressing.

1956 Brigitte Bardo makes ballet flats all the rage in the film *And God Created Woman*. Vertically challenged men rejoice.

1960 Control-top panty hose and girdles replace the chastity belt to keep a woman's sexual desires and muffin top in check.

1980 The Golden Girls popularize shoulder pads to cry on.

1990 The first water bra makes a splash, giving women one more thing to worry about leaking in the bedroom.

Future fashion inventions that will make being single even more awesome

X-ray sunglassses to see right through guys' lies, big and small.

A cocktail ring that actually rings when you need to excuse yourself from a boring conversation.

Shoes equipped with GPS (guy prowling system) to whisk you to the nearest place packed with gorgeous, available men.

A capelet that flies you to the head of the line once you arrive at said destination.

Underwire taps for your bra, allowing you to eavesdrop from across a crowded bar.

Evening bags equipped with refrigeration for stowing rum on the run.

Hoodies that function as hair dryers so you can multi-task while doing your makeup and finally be ready on time.

Tank tops with adjustable sleeves so you no longer have to complain you're cold.

Mood rings that literally adjust your mood to get you through a barrage of bad boy days.

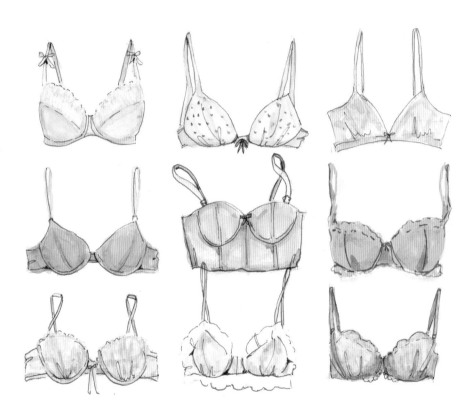

The Bra Code

A proper foundation for girls' night out, as written in accordance with Barneys Law (That is, Barneys New York, the venerable department store with Simon Doonan at the helm. Not Barney Stinson, the skirt-chaser who masterminded *The Bro Code* and wore the same suit for nine seasons on *How I Met Your Mother*). Gather your besties, cross your heart, and vow never to let your spirits sag, droop, or hang below your knees, even if nobody offers to buy you drinks after you spent two hours flat ironing your hair.

"I,____[your name]____, solemnly swear to lift, boost, and support my girls through fits of hormonal rage; tell them if they happen to be flirting with colossal boobs; never call dibs on the only top-drawer hottie in sight; and never let any man unfasten, unhook, or undo our friendship."

*Famous Bra Code pioneers: Lucy and Ethel, Thelma and Louise, Mary-Kate and Ashley, and Salt-N-Pepa.

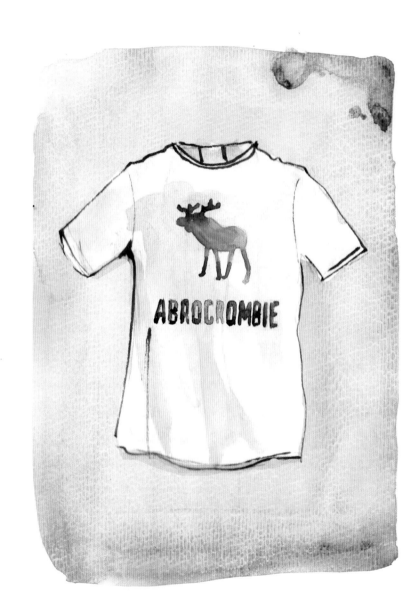

Brocabulary

*ab*rocrombie
A prepster bro who wears too much cologne and boat shoes with no socks whenever possible.

backstreet *bro*
A bro who sells you a designer knock-off on the corner of 5th and Market.

*bro*activ® solution
What to use on your face when bro-induced stress makes your skin break out.

*bro*be
The silk robe a bro slips into all Hugh Hefner-like when he wants to feel more comfortable at his place.

*bro*bituary
The announcement you make to all your friends when you're no longer dating a bro and you want them to know he's dead to you.

*bro*bsessive compulsive disorder
As suffered by the bro who alphabetizes the canned goods in his cupboards, makes you squeegee his shower after every use, and won't let you eat crackers in his bed.

*bro*ccasion jewelry
Jewelry gifted to you by a bro who will soon be planning one very scandalous boys' trip without you.

*bro*calepsy
A common condition that causes a bro to fall asleep immediately after sex.

*bro*dazzler
A bro who embellishes all of his stories, making his life appear much more glamorous and star-studded than it really is.

bro DD
A form of A.D.D. that ensures no bro can function or give eye contact in the presence of double Ds.

bro d'oeuvre
The bro you meet for cocktails before going on a dinner date with someone else.

bro dry
When your male hair stylist says the sexy blow dry he gave you calls for a night on the town—with him. (*"I thought he was gay but then he surprised me with a shampoo and bro dry."*)

WHAT'S A BRO? You'll know him by his obnoxious high five and unwavering faith in his own awesomeness, real or imagined.

bro dysmorphic syndrome
A bro who's the emotional equivalent of the fashion industry—fickle, elitist, and always setting unrealistic standards for you. Side effects of BDS are similar to what you feel while flipping through a glossy magazine: longing for lipo and wishing you had model-perfect parts.

*bro*hair sweater
A bro whose torso and back are covered in hair, creating the illusion of a chunky-knit sweater even while shirtless.

*bro*hawk
A hairstyle that a bro gets when he feels the need to test your love and devotion.

*bro*hemian
A bro with a free-spirited, shower-every-third-day kind of style. *("Not sure I'm feeling his brohemian vibe. Think he would look better on Kate Hudson.")*

*bro*incidence
When you find out the bro you're dating is friends with other bros you've also dated.

brooks *bro*
The bro in the pin-stripe Brooks Brothers suit who tries to sell you an insurance plan over dinner and write off your entire relationship as a business expense.

*bro*muda triangle
Where you can expect to find a bro after telling him you love him too soon.

*bro*phylactic
Your best defense against diseases spread by *bro*miscuity and nymph*bro*mania.

bro pitt
The best-looking bro you've ever seen in the flesh.

bro-polar
Used to describe a bro that blows hot and cold. *("Pass the Brozdc, my new crush is depressingly bro-polar.")*

*bro*punzel
Any bro whose hair is longer than your skirt.

*bro*tographer
A predatory bro who pretends to work in the fashion industry just to get close to the models.

*bro*quet
An apologetic arrangement left to wilt at your doorstep by a bro, made up of the cheapest possible combination of carnations and baby's breath or cauliflower and broccoli.

brosacea
Skin irritation caused by making out with a bro who has intense beard stubble. *("Ugh, my face is all red and irritated post-makeout. Do you have anything over-the-counter to treat Brosacea?")*

brotique
A store where you shop only because you know good-looking bros will be there.

broveralls
A denim bib worn by Jethro bro.

broverted justice
An agency out to prevent much older bros from preying on much younger women.

brozilian wax
A treatment wherein a bro's nether regions get hot-waxed into porn-shorn oblivion.

dermabrosion
The process of removing or gradually sloughing off a flaky bro.

esbrodrilles
A tightly woven group of bros who come out in full force during Daisy Dukes and miniskirt weather. *("The Marina is hoppin' today. Must be esbrodrille season.")*

febroary 14
A twenty-four-hour test of sanity and strength for any woman hopelessly in love with a clueless bro.

little bro peep
The bro who clocks hundreds of hours in front of his computer watching online porn.

metbrosexual
The ambiguously straight bro who's always the first to notice when you change your nail polish or trim your bangs.

superbro sunday
A national shopping holiday for the wives and girlfriends of football-fanatic bros.

unibro
A bro who obviously doesn't give a pluck and has one continuous overgrown eyebrow to show for it.

zebro
A bro solely interested in *ze sex* whose motives are completely black and white.

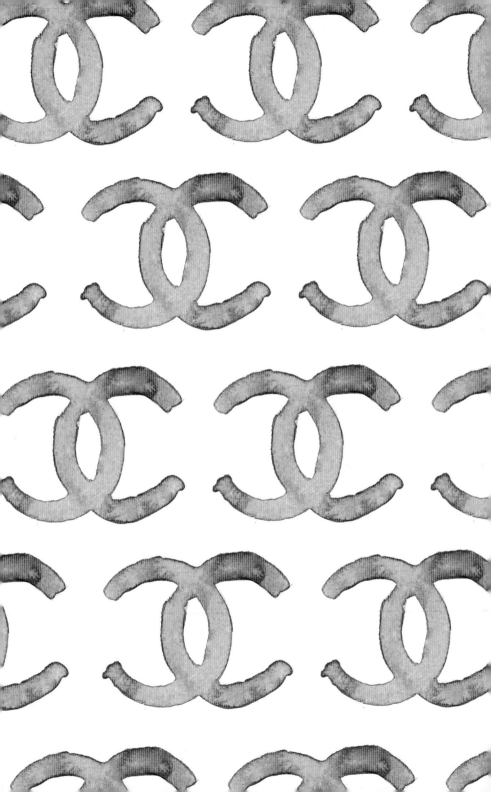

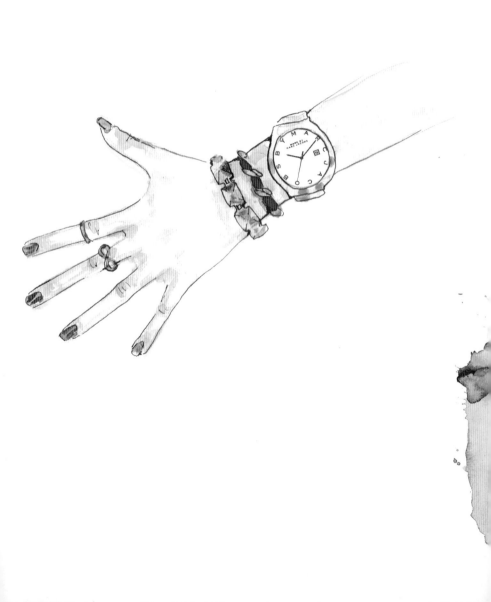

Rule 9

Love is like a Marc Jacobs show. There's no telling when it will actually happen, but it's definitely not going to happen when everybody told you it was going to happen.

These things never run on schedule.

Rule 10

Always wear a glimmer of hope on a first date.

Dresses that will be submerged under the dinner table for most of the evening should be adorned with shimmering, face-illuminating jewelry. Also chic: touchable cashmere, peek-a-boo lace, wispy silks, off-the-shoulder sweaters, and any accessory that reflects your travels and personal history. An outfit is doing its job when it asserts your identity and leads to sparkling conversation.

Rule 11

Don't be seduced by tall, strapping, punishingly gorgeous heels that are sure to knock you off balance.

Beware of the great-looking jerk you can't be yourself around, and the one who makes early declarations of love that make you feel like you can touch the sky. You won't stay that high forever. Sorry to burst your bubble skirt.

Rule 12

Take risks, glorious risks!

You know how everyone who's anyone is willing to look ridiculous for a punk-themed Met Gala? Similarly, you have to risk looking like a fool for romance. You're not always going to get it right. People may stare. But at least you made it worth their while.

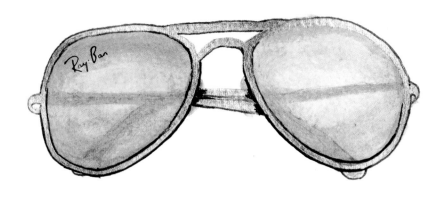

Rule 13

If there's one thing Maverick and Ice Man taught us, it's that aviators are h-o-t.

There's something so thrilling, so dashing, so utterly *Highway to the Danger Zone* about them. Especially the mirrored ones by Ray-Ban, and the ones who fly you to Paris on a whim in their private jets.

Rule 14

Ignore *un*dress codes perpetuated by men.

You're not expected to sleep with him on the third date. Regarding physical intimacy, it's perfectly okay to be stingy with samples just like the girls behind the department store. As the saying goes, *"Why buy the $745 jar of skin caviar when you can get the little trial packets for free?"*

Rule 15

Beware the Peter Pan epidemic.

Not the blouses with the little rounded sleeves, but the guys who are emotionally stunted and will always find a reason to keep you at a distance in Never-Neverland because the responsibility of a relationship is a real buzzkill. Be on the lookout for gummy vitamins in his cabinets and quarters from his mother in the mail (she worries he doesn't do laundry).

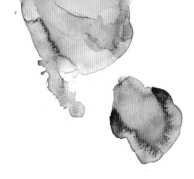

Rule 16

Let him move in with you prematurely and he may start
to resemble an apathetic old sales lady, saying things
like, *"That's not my department,"* or *"Go ask someone else, I'm
on a break"* when asked to do the dishes.

He might also leave toenail clippings in your bed or blow his nose on
your 3,000-count Egyptian cotton sheets. To ensure that living with
him won't prove to be a total waste of closet space, give him a simple
test: Hide the towels and toilet paper, leave one of your scarves within
reach (preferably a cheap one you never liked much anyway), and
see what ensues.

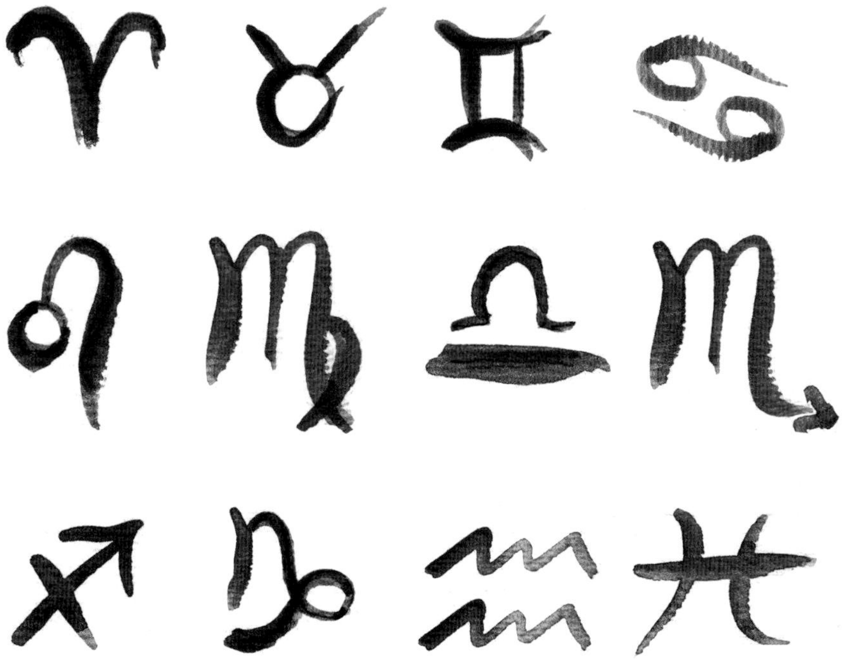

Fash-strology

Surely you believe everything written in *Cosmo*, but what about what's written in the cosmos? Here's who you should be cohabitating in bliss with, as written in the stars.

ARIES March 21 to April 19
Best matches: Leo, Sagittarius, Gemini, Aquarius

TAURUS April 20 to May 20
Best matches: Virgo, Pisces, Scorpio, Capricorn

GEMINI May 21 to June 20
Best matches: Sagittarius, Libra, Aquarius, Leo

CANCER June 21 to July 22
Best matches: Pisces, Capricorn, Scorpio, Virgo

LEO July 23 to August 22
Best matches: Sagittarius, Aquarius, Aries, Libra

VIRGO August 23 to September 22
Best matches: Taurus, Scorpio, Capricorn, Pisces

LIBRA September 23 to October 22
Best matches: Leo, Gemini, Aquarius, Sagittarius

SCORPIO October 23 to November 21
Best matches: Virgo, Pisces, Taurus, Cancer, Capricorn

SAGITTARIUS November 22 to December 21
Best matches: Libra, Leo, Gemini, Aries, Aquarius

CAPRICORN December 22 to January 19
Best matches: Scorpio, Virgo, Pisces, Taurus

AQUARUIS January 20 to February 18
Best matches: Gemini, Sagittarius, Libra, Aries

PISCES February 19 to March 20
Best matches: Scorpio, Capricorn, Cancer, Taurus

Rule 17

Sleep with a married man and lose your right to rock
anything bearing the words Citizens of Humanity.

Très inhumane. Did we mention all husband-lifters will be prosecuted to
the fullest extent of karmic laws?

BURBERRY

6012 Pandoma Rd
Columbus, OH 43204
Telephone: (614) 292-6104

Salesperson: JAMIE No. 6813

SILK SCA 8913476800	250.00
BELFORT DRESS M 8917222543	712.00
PUMPS RED 1 NB BARNSFLD3892	350.00

Subtotal

Subtotal	$1312.00
Tax	$121.67
Total	$1433.67

Rule 18

Keep every receipt.

Some (okay, lots of) guys have a way of conveniently forgetting (okay, denying) things they've said or written in the past. Keep a journal and delete nothing. These paper trails will prevent you from glamorizing his memory, or feeling insane when he says, *"Sorry, I don't remember events A, B, C . . . X, Y, and Z."*

Closet confession

Enough time had flown by since Riley and Ben's breakup where she found herself missing him and forgetting why they'd broken up in the first place. This condition is known as *glamnesia*—it's basically a temporary memory lapse that occurs when an ex hasn't been in your life for more than two years, causing you to glamorize his good side and forget all the reasons you broke up with him in the first place. The trigger is usually a string of so-so dates and unfamiliar kisses that leave you wondering what your former flame is up to. Or a rumor that he's engaged.

At work, Riley was perfectly busy and functioning like normal, but at night her glamnesia was unbearable. She'd finally gotten around to reading the book Ben had given her years prior. And she'd go to bed trying to imagine what it would be like to kiss him again.

Her mind was like a movie screen projecting all sorts of vivid images, like the time Ben said she was his "soulmate," and the time he'd surprised her with her own guitar, urging her to learn how to play with him. She missed how he marveled at her body every time she disrobed. And how he made her feel like she was the only woman he'd ever loved. Had she made a major mistake breaking up with him?

One night at happy hour, a bartender serendipitously overserved Riley and she mustered enough courage to text Ben to find out if the buzz about his recent engagement was true. When he texted back, *"Hi beautiful, not engaged,"* her pulse quickened. They exchanged a few texts and emails and met for dinner and cocktails a couple of days later.

Truths contained in this book are as blunt as Anna Wintour's bob.

Rule 19

Something is *très* peculiar when all of his exes look alike, as if they were culled from an assembly line.

Dear Chris Klein, you had excellent taste in Ginnifer Goodwin and Katie Holmes, but how did you kiss the former without thinking of the latter? It's all a little *sketchballs* if you ask us (hello lifetime girlfriend replacement program).

*Four-inch heels not only give you an enviably long-stemmed look, they make you four times hotter to men because you're four times slower to escape their sexual advances.

Rule 20

The higher the stilettos, the closer to closure.

The best way to get over a man is to get under his skin, simply by making your legs look amazing. Plus, you literally become the bigger person, taking the high road in your Giuseppe Zanottis.

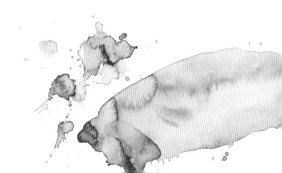

Rule 21

Thanks to a bevy of boyfriend trends (slouchy jeans, oversized cardigans, and even watches) you now have an excuse to scour the men's department for your next boyfriend.

And then once you find him, you can buy him a gift . . . for yourself.

Rule 22

When it comes to your makeup and your boyfriends, your mother will always second-guess your choices. Try not to get upset, it's her maternal duty.

Perhaps there's no pleasing her because you're so great. Or maybe he really is horrible. Splashing your face with ice water every morning will help you see things more clearly while also tightening your pores.

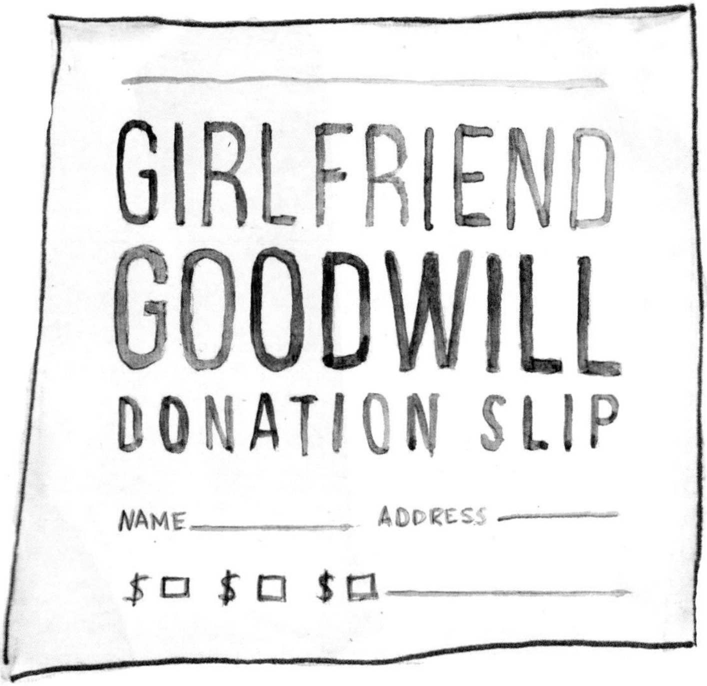
GIRLFRIEND
GOODWILL
DONATION SLIP
NAME
ADDRESS
$ $ $

Rule 23

Every spring, declutter your heart and your closet to make room for better things.

Divide and conquer your romantic options in three piles [*hell yes/ hell no/ hell, why not?*]. Ask yourself a few key questions: Am I keeping him out of obligation or expectation? Am I saving him just in case? Am I holding onto something broken hoping I'll fix it one day? In the event you don't realize he's a keeper until it's too late and you've already written him off, your charitable donation to womankind will not go unnoticed.

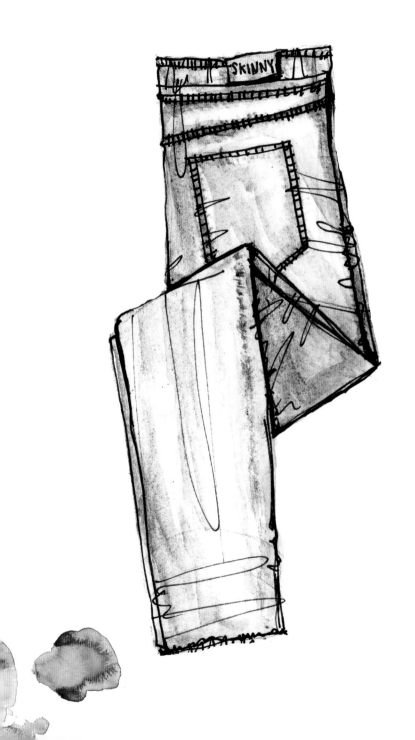

Rule 24

Relationships and skinny jeans should allow room
to breathe.

Being exceptionally tight is one thing, but suffocation is another. Don't
let him cut off your circulation from the rest of the world.

Rule 25

His pet nickname for you should be one-of-a-kind and
custom-made.

Finding out from his roommate that he calls all of his flames Babydoll?
Priceless. Someone should tell him to button it.

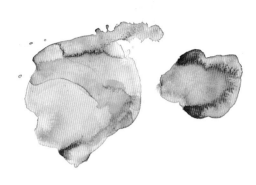

Rule 26

Thanks to Rent the Runway and Bag Borrow or Steal, there's no shame in bringing a loaner bag or boyfriend to a big event where you want to turn heads.

Disclaimer: You must always ask permission to borrow someone else's man for the night and return him in the exact same condition he was loaned to you.

hello hello hello
hello hello hello
hello hello hello
hello hello hello
hello hello hello
hello hello hello
hello hello hello
hello hello hello
hello hello hello
hello hello hello

Rule 27

The etiquette for talking to a living mannequin is like that of a sample sale. You can use your shoulders to make your way through the crowd, but no shoving, elbowing, or trampling small children to get to him first.

Try to determine if he's taken or available, like you would a fitting room (don't just awkwardly barge into his space). If you don't see any signs of a ring or a tanline where his ring should be, you may proceed. Not sure what to say? A simple "hello" is the ultimate statement-maker. If he's interested, available, and equipped with a personality, you can count on him to take care of the rest.

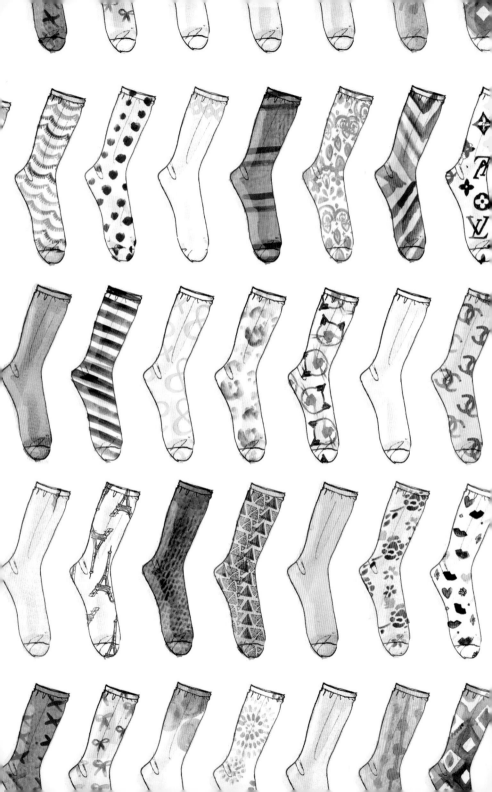

Most of your socks are single and loving it.

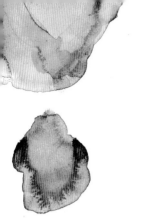

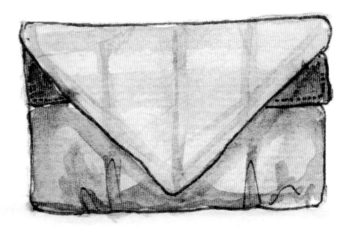

Rule 28

For better or worse, style will always love you.

We hold these truths to be self-evident: that there will never be a shortage of dazzling studs at Tiffany & Co., that there will always be a Brian Atwood clutch to have and to hold, and that no man will ever kiss your feet like a pair of Jimmy Choos.

Rule 29

Uninterested guys are as transparent as stripper heels.

Do you get one-word responses when you text him? Does he hook up with you right before disappearing for weeks? Or says things like *"We'll catch up soon,"* when you could simply catch up right now? Clearly he doesn't know what he's missing out on and we don't like the idea of you squandering your fabulosity on that kind of ding dong.

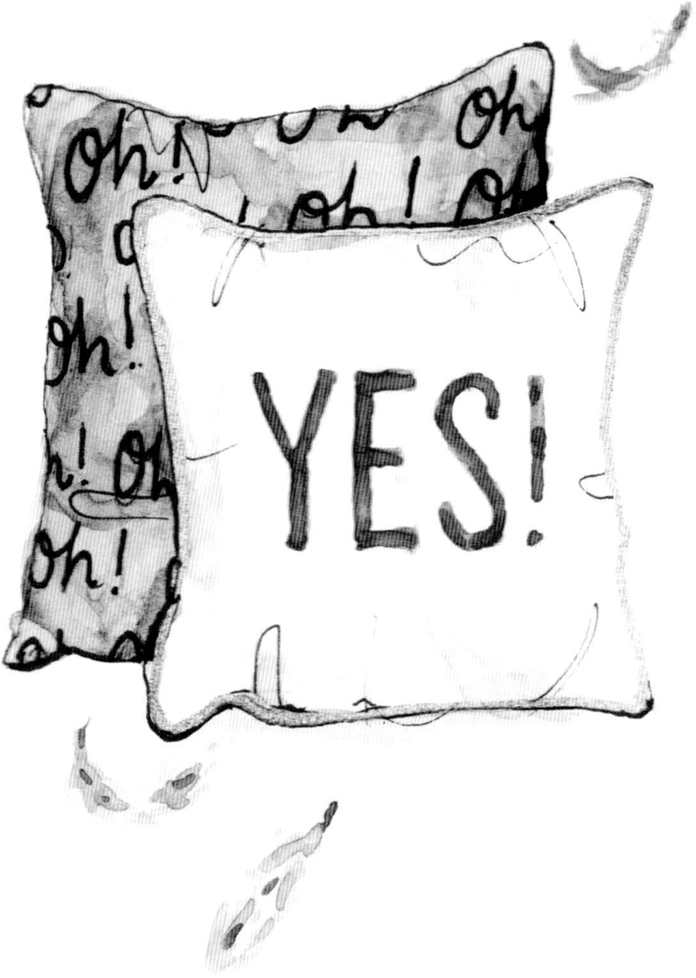
Oh!
YES!

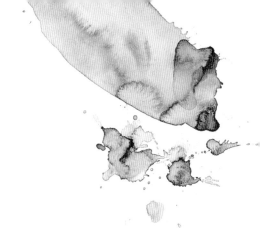

Rule 30

Never stage a passion show.

Putting on a motion picture–worthy performance in the boudoir, complete with costume and sound effects, sets into motion a terrible chain of events. You squeal with ecstasy. He thinks that weird thing he's doing to you is fireworks-spectacular, and the next woman who comes along must also suffer. *Quel* horror.

*Wait! Before you completely give up on a man who can't locate your love button, remember most women can't even locate their own waist. It's a few inches higher than you think, right under the rib cage—that's where a belt should cinch your dress.

Rule 31

Allow yourself a full thirty days before
making any hasty decisions and putting him
back on the shelf for someone else to snap up.

How to break off an engagement, per standard store
return policies.

hey
girl

MEET RYAN GOSLING 2.0,
HE'S FOLLOWING YOUR DREAM
GUY INSPIRATION BOARD
ON PINTEREST.

Rule 32

Lose the impossible shopping list.

It's no secret that some women carry around a long list of nonnegotiable qualities they want in a husband. Good with kids? *Check.* Loves to cook? *Check.* Mom and Dad adore him? *Check.* But if you're holding out for someone who looks just like Ryan Gosling with broader shoulders, better abs, and whiter teeth, there's a good chance you're setting yourself up for disappointment of pageant-hair proportions.

TALL ✓
DARK ✓
HANDSOME ✓

NOW'S YOUR CHANCE TO CREATE A SHOPPING LIST FULL OF NOT-SO-RIDICULOUS *Non negotiables*

Rule 33

Never let a guy interfere with your spending habits.

This includes time spent aging by the phone waiting for his call, gas spent driving by his house to quiet your nagging suspicions, and money spent on flowers (sent to you, by you) *à la* Cher Horowitz in *Clueless*.

Rule 34

Want the latest status symbol on your arm? Prepare to be waitlisted.

Just as there are It bags, there are It boys who are coveted just because they've been publicized, editorialized, and celebritized in all the latest magazines. If you want to date a celeb, heed the laws of nature: Reality stars always get engaged to other reality stars (they're more likely to be recognized in public together that way), supermodels attract musicians who share their love of eyeliner, and beauty queens compete to take the last names of nominally famous professional athletes. What nobody tells you is that the swirling infidelity rumors are what keep these poor girls skinny. Size 1 is the loneliest number indeed.

Dear Editrix,

I'm pretty sure I was born to be on the red carpet with Giuliana Rancic and Ryan Seacrest. Is it wrong to take the easy route by dating celebrities?

—Hollywood Hopeful

Dear Hopeful,

You'll soon find that having a celebrity on your arm is like wearing a dress entirely made of dark chocolate: everyone is going to want a piece. Have your fling, but try to avoid becoming head-over-skirt in love with anyone making headlines on page six.

—Editrix

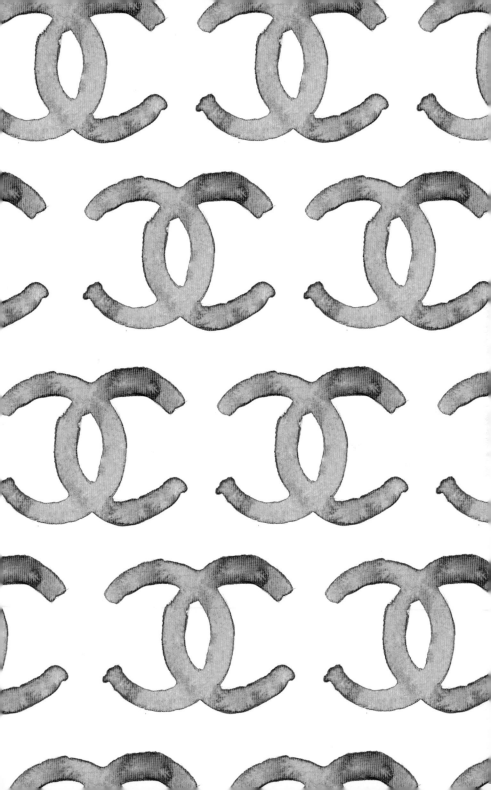

Closet confession

Even though Marni wasn't exactly a sports fan (often referring to team uniforms as "outfits"), she'd heard plenty of wild rumors about professional athletes and their assorted sexual conquests. Her friend Haley had once dated Mike Maddie, a famous pitcher who threw her out of his bed and into his closet when "his parents" unexpectedly showed up at his door ("his parents" . . . *riiiiiight*). Meanwhile, Marni's coworker Erica had once left a bar at closing time with World Series champion Paul Barnes, who was notorious for getting buck naked in a batting stance and modestly saying things like, *"Take a picture, you're about to [dirty verb] Paul Barnes."*

Needless to say, when Marni met major league babe Derk Smith in the flesh at a fund-raising event, she knew what she might be getting into; it's just that all common sense had faded like semipermanent hair color the moment she locked eyes with him. They exchanged flirtatious conversation and phone numbers over drinks, and he left for spring training the next morning, determined to see her upon his triumphant return. His texts and televised appearances kept her interested for the next few weeks, which was just enough time to hit up Google to find out pretty much everything about him.

As to be expected, all the rumors about the notorious womanizer lived online in great detail. Playboy bunnies. *Maxim* models. World's sexiest actresses. Marni convinced herself that she was too civilian for him, and that she should bail before getting hurt (or getting STDs), but when Derk called in his sexy voice to firm up their plans, she agreed to go out with him anyway <secret shame>. She'd never been out with a man whose body parts were insured before.

They ended up going to a hip hotel lounge where he confided he was "infatuated" by her and her off-the-shoulder shirt (he assumed she wasn't wearing a bra). Marni describes the whole experience as out-of-body. Here was this well-known guy she'd watched on television so many times, making goo-goo eyes at her. And here was this cocktail server who kept bending over to exaggerate her cleavage every time she poured Derk's drink, and these random guys interrupting their date to ask for autographs and photos, and these star-struck girls descending out of nowhere trying to make fast friends (one even asked if she could move in with Marni).

Later that night, around 2 a.m., hotel staff giggled and stared as Marni and Derk made their way up to his penthouse suite, where jars of expensive skincare lined the bathroom counters and hundred dollar bills were spilling out of the nightstand onto the floor. A lesser woman would have grabbed one (he never would have known it was missing); instead, they made out like seventh graders until 3 a.m. and she snuck out just before the sun came up, even though he wanted to go to breakfast.

He continued to text and call for the next few weeks, saying things like, *"I've been referencing our night together"* (a sexual innuendo, of course). That was around the time she read in *US Weekly* he was rumored to be involved with an up-and-coming Hollywood pop starlet. He'd been photographed by paparazzi with the Disney singer-actress leaving a nightclub with a team sweatshirt over his head.

In the end, these things wore Marni out. Never fear, her time with Derk wasn't a total waste of lip gloss. Derk had picked up a few key styling ideas from her, as evidenced by photos taken of him at a drag-themed team charity event in the weeks that followed. The look? A familiar-looking off-the-shoulder shirt. *Très* scary but also *très* flattering, no?

Rule 35

Swap 'til you drop.

Every now and then, have a swapping party where each invitee brings a guy she likes-but-doesn't-love-anymore and is willing to amicably part with. Be sure to lay down the rules in advance. No musty duds and no Indian gives. Invitations should boldly read *B.Y.O.B.* (bring your old beau).

Rule 36

It's never a good sign if he says he's not into labels
(particularly the very exclusive Boyfriend-Girlfriend label).

A cop-out like this could leave you duped for months. Don't be fooled by
an ongoing *faux*-lationship.

Rule 37

Boyfriends and fur must be cruelty-free per PETA standards.

No pushing you. No shoving you. No hitting you. No excuses.

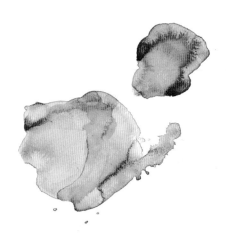

Rule 38

Never drop everything and move for a guy, especially to
a foreign country where you'll suffer bouts of anxiety,
depression, and deprivation when you miss all of your friends
and don't know how to ask for anything cute in your size.

You have better things to spend your Euros on than grief counseling.

Rule 39

You can't tailor a man to your specifications, no matter
how hard you try.

Honestly, some men have even tried to change themselves without luck.
Love him as he is or move along. You wouldn't buy a skirt that's too small
hoping it will one day fit, would you?

How to upgrade your man's style
(without him noticing)

Take baby steps. Start by replacing his old underwear and socks, see how he reacts, then work your way onto bigger things, like jackets and pants.

Keep it positive. It's as simple as saying, *"You'd look amazing in that"* as you pass a store window together.

Replace his grooming products and leave them in the shower. Or try planting a tube of eye cream on his counter.

Is your guy grimey? Offer to shampoo his hair, then massage his scalp, or give him a candlelit facial to combat his breakouts.

Back full of hair? Are you willing to be the one who rubs Nair on it?

Rough hands? Moisturize and massage them, one at a time, while sitting in the car at a red light.

*Whatever you do, don't throw away any of his belongings. This is the kind of thing that always gets Marie Barone into trouble on *Everybody Loves Raymond*.

A prayer to Saint Laurent for divine intervention

Oh venerable patron saint of sartorial miracles, I know what I'm about to say is going to make me sound like a vain girlfriend and possibly also a very bad person. Please forgive me and please grant me the willpower to bite my tongue when my boyfriend dresses himself. I'm not sure how much longer I can take the whole white socks with dark suits thing. And please don't let him wear those awful amphibious shoes with the gnarly webbed toes to my parent's dinner party. *Amen.*

Rule 40

Never fight over a man as though he's the last gift with purchase.

Assuredly, there are 3.4 billion men in the world. Factoring in that 340 million are gay or don't know it yet, and 567,025 think they're God's gifts, that still leaves plenty for you to work with.

Rule 41

Keep your hang-ups in the closet.

What's the use in spending three hours getting ready if you're going to point out all the things you don't like about yourself over cocktails?

Rule 42

Just because you have a credit card doesn't mean you have to buy his *merde*.

Isn't it marvelous how *sh*t* always sounds better in French?

Closet confession: Paris edition

There's something about traveling to a foreign country that makes American women feel sexy and fearless, a dangerous combination that finds them justifying scandalously expensive purchases and scandalously shady Casanovas they wouldn't dare indulge in back home.

Rewind to 2005. While feasting curbside on the *Champs-Élysées* and salivating over their *shoppings*, Emily and Nicole were approached by two Parisian men who'd strolled by their table several (million) times. Emily got along marvelously with the harmless, overweight one who rambled on about his beautiful wife in broken English. Nicole, a Texas-bred beauty who spoke near-fluent French with a southern drawl, was instantly smitten by Jacques, the hunky one who took bites of her snails and sips of her chardonnay while whispering, *"Est-ce que ce vin va bien avec la sexe?"* (roughly translated as, *"Does this wine go with sex?"*). Maybe it was something in the way Jacques peppered his speech with question marks. Maybe it was something in the *fromage*. By the time the peaches *flambé* had arrived at their table, Nicole was smitten and Emily was left to play wing woman and make small talk with Jacques's married friend until the wee hours.

After finishing dinner, the four of them decided to hit up a show at Moulin Rouge, which made Emily uncomfortable for two reasons: watching topless women dance while in the company of strange men did not seem like the best idea, and she really felt her Euros would have been better spent on the handbag she'd spotted in the window at Printemps, the Parisian equivalent of Bloomingdale's.

During the cab ride home with a canoodling Nicole and Jaqcues, Emily poked her head out of the window to watch the alluring city (an emblem for romance, magic, and mystery) recede into the background. Never content with background anything, Nicole tried to take Jacques upstairs to her tiny hotel bed. When her efforts were brutally rebuffed by the nosy innkeeper watching over the lobby, Nicole told Emily she would stay outside for a few minutes to bid Jacques *bon voyage* and snag an authentic French kiss.

The next morning, when Nicole finally floated through the hotel's front doors with a grin on her face and glazed look in her eye, Emily was on the phone with one hot, panicked tear running down her cheek. She had been trying, unsuccessfully, to describe Jacques to the police with her pocket translator, all the while wondering if she'd be able to find her way back to America in the event something unspeakable had happened to her adorable French-speaking pal.

Quel nightmare.

Thankfully, all was not lost and the adventure continued. When the girls boarded their flight home a week later, poor Nicole still hadn't heard from Jacques after spending the night with him and thinking he'd call. Perhaps it's not a stretch to say that all men speak the same language, regardless of their country of origin. It's quite possible *"I'll call you"* universally means *"Bahahahahaha."*

WANTED

Fashionable single female seeks sensible flats to sweep her off her feet. Must be prepared to endure long walks, on the beach and other assorted adventures on foot. Seriously comfortable inquiries only.

Rule 43

Don't be so quick to trust a guy who wears more jewelry than you.

Particularly an ankle bracelet that monitors his whereabouts. But, you never know, maybe his parole officer is dashing and available?

*And don't be so quick to trust a guy who throws lingerie parties.

Rule 44

Always make an effort to appear effortless, just like Kate Moss.

If you're relaxed, self-assured, and radiating laidback-cool, you're guaranteed to draw droves of men like frugalistas to a Half Yearly Sale. Moss is proof that if you put enough care into looking like you don't care, you'll achieve muse status: Johnny Depp will want to date you, women will want to be you, and pets and paparazzi will follow you everywhere you go.

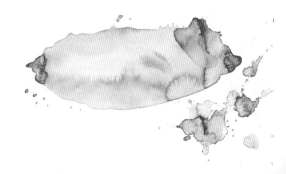

Rule 45

If he's not capable of looking after your purse while you excuse yourself to go to the restroom, you probably have no future together.

Harsh, we know. But if he won't hold your baby Chloé, Stella, or Céline, or if he leaves it unattended in the presence of strangers, he certainly won't be capable of watching children, pets, or anything of living, breathing value down the road.

Rule 46

Following a breakup, hide all weapons of self-destruction, including rusty kitchen scissors, tweezers, and magnifying mirrors, which can lead to the obliteration of eyebrows and violent extraction of innocent pores.

Best to keep depilatories away from your favorite fur vest while you're at it.

Rule 47

The minute a man makes your butt feel big is the minute
you should make like panty hose (and run!).

Does he track your weight like an issue of *In Touch Weekly?* Life's too
short to commit to anyone or anything requiring you to give up grilled
cheese sandwiches or suck in your stomach at all times. Throw him to the
curb and instantly lose 225 pounds. (Remember to lift with your legs.)

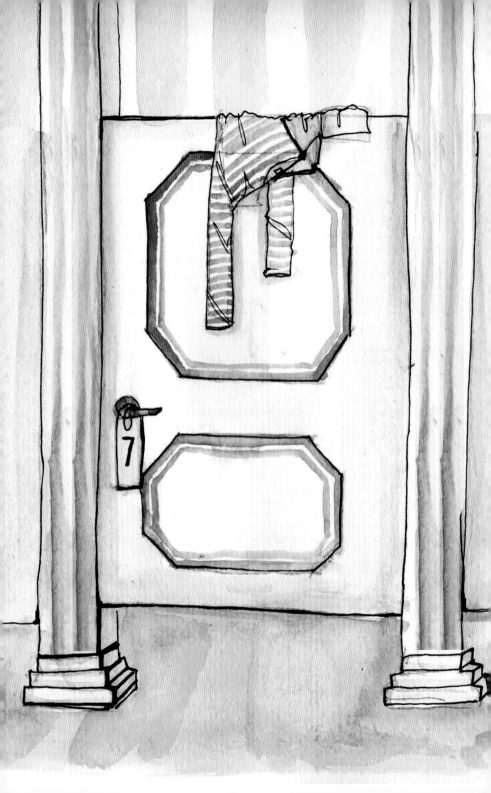

Rule 48

Never let a guy or a pushy sales person coerce you to get a room before you're ready or talk you into something you may regret.

Aggressive dates are not unlike aggressive sales people, forcing themselves on you with a hard sell, putting you in an awkward position, and saying things you want to hear just to seal the deal. A prized few may even pretend they don't understand your language when faced with the word "*no.*"

I DON'T
SPEAK ITALIAN
BUT I
DO SPEAK
MOSCHINO

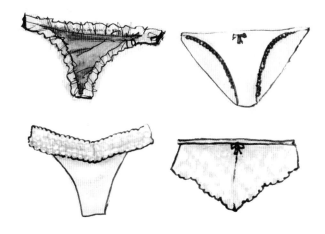

Classic panty lines

Did you get those jeans on sale? Because they're 100 percent off at my place.

Your dress would look better on my floor.

Can I read your T-shirt in braille?

It's cold. Let me wrap my [*body part*] around you like a scarf.

Let's make like fabric softener and Snuggle.

Do you wash your clothes with Windex? Because I can see myself in your pants.

Is your body's name Visa? Cuz it's everywhere I wanna be.

*If you don't believe that some men use the exact same line on every maiden who walks by, set up camp in the mall and watch the guys in the kiosks selling flat irons and fake ponytails go to work.

Rule 49

Be mindful of emerging trends.

Trend alert! He's withholding his home number, has juice boxes and Happy Meal toys in the backseat of his car, and is never available on the weekends or key holidays. These are the distinguishing marks of a married man with family obligations.

Rule 50

Just as fashion is cyclical, your emotions are dictated by the seasons (resort/pre-spring/spring/summer/pre-fall/fall/ winter).

Seasonal memory triggers, like the smell of Christmas trees, burning firewood, and Gucci Guilty Pour Homme cologne, can bring back flashes of the past, which explains the sudden nostalgia for your long-gone ex on a crowded train. This too shall pass. Eat some dark chocolate, watch some *Sex and the City*, and call us in the morning.

Rule 51

Think age appropriate.

It's only a matter of time before chasing frat boys and wearing tiny denim shorts makes you look completely out of touch. Rule breaker we love: Demi Moore.

FOREVER AND EVER

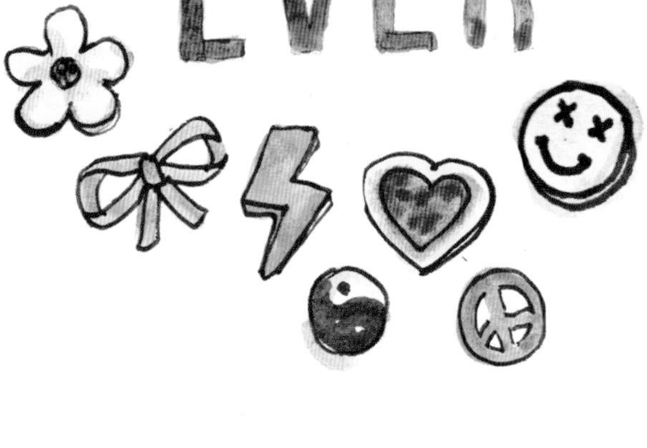

Start antiaging your game now because the more you wear SPF and moisturize your neck and elbows, the more ambiguous your age will remain and the more romantic options you'll have for the rest of your life.

Do invest in silk or satin pillowcases to prevent your skin from being wrinkled like a Shar-Pei while you sleep.

Do take care not to overapply eye cream, as it can actually backfire and cause puffy eyes.

Don't make a habit of drinking from a straw or bottle, which can exaggerate the parenthesis lines around your mouth.

Don't tense up your jaw and throat while working out. This can make your neck look stringy and face look drawn long-term.

*How young is too young to date? Divide your age by two and add seven.

Rule 52

Versatility is *très* important.

Can you take him anywhere, dressed up or down? Or will he whine and tug on your sleeve when he wants to leave the most glamorous social event of the season to play Xbox?

Rule 53

Relationships always look better on the model.

How many times have you presumed, from a reasonable distance, that all of your married friends have perfect unions and are happier than you? Meanwhile, they have moments when they long for their days as solo-flying single girls. Even Gisele Bündchen thinks the grass is greener from time to time. Oh, who are we kidding? Tom Brady's the best-looking guy on the planet, and she can eat whatever she wants and it all goes to her boobs. Her life's perfect. Let's all try to be happy for her.

Rule 54

Lust finds you naked more than you're dressed, so you'll never have to worry about what to wear so long as there's whipped cream in the fridge.

One to try: fat-free Cool Whip.

Buyer beware

The Sneaker Runs around with lots of women.

The Croc Can't believe a word he says.

The Ugg Could have sworn he was better looking?

The Sweater Drips profusely when asked where he was last night.

The Loafer Lives on your couch and eats all your food.

The Jumper Wants to leap in too soon.

The Mule Stubborn as those last five pounds.

The Flip-Flop Your favorite mistake.

The Turtleneck Overextends his neck to ogle other women.

The Shrug Ever met anyone so indecisive?

The Wedge Comes between you and your friends or family.

The Long John Ouch, overrated.

The Suspender Leaves your Saturday night plans in suspense.

The Clog Obstructs you from getting on with your life.

The Onesie Don't let him get away.

*Prices you pay may vary.

Rule 55

You are what you sleep in.

Are you sexy in satin? Or frumpy in flannel?

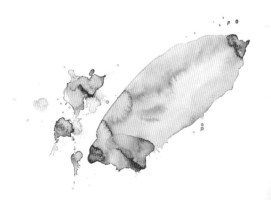

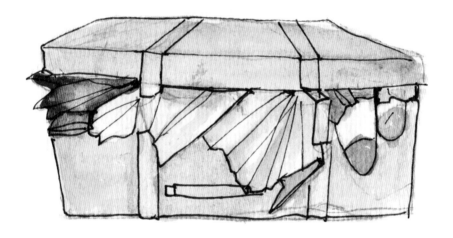

Rule 56

Past lovers are the kind of baggage that should fold away neatly where you don't have to constantly be reminded of them.

Spoiler alert! If he's saying unkind things about his ex, or revealing all of the gory details of their relationship, you know he'll be doing the same to you in the future.

Rule 57

Shopping and dating are two things you don't want to do while intoxicated or you may end up taking home something or someone you have lukewarm feelings for.

Waking up to someone you barely know can be dreadful. Shame on the entertainment-minded date who treats you like a reality show contestant, giving you lots of champagne and not much to eat in hopes you'll do something out of the ordinary that he'll get to watch.

Rule 58

Once a cheetah, always a cheetah.

Fact: The only cheetah worthy of your time is the one printed on your Dolce & Gabbana bag.

Closet confession

I t was early summer and the smell of Coppertone and citrusy perfume filled the air. Jessica had just moved from rainy Seattle to sunny California in order to live with Zack, her boyfriend of two years. She took nothing but a suitcase with her—brimming with high hopes and high fashion.

Getting settled into Zack's luxury condo was all very exciting in a clean slate kind of way. Zack had cheated on Jessica months prior, but it seemed as though all of that was behind them. He was determined to earn back her trust, and she was eager to get married before turning thirty-five next year. At some point, he'd even given her his email password as proof of his newfound fidelity. Just the fact he wanted her to have it was all she really needed. Things were finally sailing along smoothly.

Cue the *Jaws* theme song *<dun-dun dun-dun dun-dun>*.

The couple had been living together for less than a month when Jessica started experiencing an emotional tsunami (killer waves of doubt). Zack had left her alone while he was away on a business trip and his ex-wife, whom he'd also cheated on in the past, was repeatedly calling and leaving messages for him on the home phone: *<Beep!>* *"I need to speak with you urgently. Call me back, as soon as you can, okay?"* *<Click!>*.

Jessica's mind started racing: Could Zack be sleeping with his ex-wife? Was he really out of town on business, or was that a lie?

At the time, Jessica thought this may be her imagination running wild, but in hindsight, it was actually her intuition kicking into overdrive. In a desperate move, she logged into Zack's email account. Deep in his archives, where he probably thought she'd never look, she found a registration email indicating Zack had opened another personal email account about a year prior.

That second account, which was foolishly programmed with the same *stud69* password, had been the one appointed for all of Zack's closeted secrets. In it, Jessica found infinite porn subscriptions, along with written exchanges from what appeared to be Zack's longtime lover, Kate, a married woman who lived nearby.

A deeper dive revealed all sorts of pantsless photos of Kate. Every email Jessica opened was progressively worse than the last, divulging how much Kate loved him, craved him, and wanted him to ravage her.

Jessica began to convulse and dry-heave in front of the computer as she read Kate's emails, screaming, *"Oh gawd, oh gawd, oh gawwwwd"* like the scene right before the *Titanic* sank. She picked up the phone and called her friend Tara who lived upstairs.

Tara arrived at the tragic scene breathless from running down a flight of stairs, just in time to stop Jessica from throwing all of Zack's hash-marked underpants over the balcony and writing profanities on his winter white bedspread with a black Sharpie.

Luckily, Tara convinced Jessica that would be a little *too* psycho, so they compromised by throwing hangers all over the closet floor after they'd packed up all of Jessica's clothes, and maxed out his air conditioner so he'd return to an enormous PG&E bill three days later.

Just then, as if on cue, Zack's ex-wife called and left another message: *<Beep!>* *"Seriously Zack, this is the last time before I go crazy. I want the stuff back that you broke in and took from the house, you selfish #%*!"* *<Click!>*.

"Ahhhh! I moved for him! He's so gross! I feel so stupid," Jessica sobbed, packing her Louis Vuitton luggage with Tasmanian Devil speed in an effort to catch the next flight back to Seattle.

Outside the building as Tara saw Jessica off, they hugged like World War II soldiers forever bonded by combat. *"I'll call you when I land,"* Jessica yelled from her cab. *"Thank you for being such a good friend!"*

For the next few months, Jessica and Tara kept in touch every day. (There is no greater bond than between women scorned.) In that time, Jessica had somehow managed to do what all women fantasize about doing under similar circumstances: save the nude photos she'd found of Kate and send them to Kate's boss via an address listed online. The plot kept thickening, just like a *Lifetime Original Movie*.

Meanwhile, when Zack returned home to the arctic chill in his condo, he called Jessica in crocodile tears. From that point on, he called her several times a day to whimper, whine, and beg her to take him back. He said he was going to start seeking help for his philandering ways by attending meetings similar to Alcoholics Anonymous, but for compulsive liars and two-timers.

As time passed and Jessica's hurt began to heal, her communication with Tara slowly came to a halt. Tara had assumed it was because Jessica wanted to move on from Zack's filthy memory.

Three months later, as Tara was waiting for the condo elevator, the doors opened with Zack and a very embarrassed Jessica inside. They were kissing and holding hands, and they walked right by Tara as if they didn't know her. It turns out Jessica had severed all contact with Tara because she knew too much.

Jessica never got married. At least, not to Zack. Their final breakup was instigated by another one of his indiscretions. The guy was a polka dot sundress, and he never changed his spots.

*Pitiful as it may sound, Zack eventually tried to date Tara, much to her horror.

Fashion editor girlfriends say the darndest things

"My heart hasn't been broken like this since Ralph Lauren dropped Polo from his name."

"You don't embrace me like my cropped shearling moto jacket does."

"Wanna do it in a Nordstrom fitting room?"

"We're naming our first born Mark Down."

"I miss you like Van Cleef would miss Arpels."

"My heart isn't a catwalk; you can't just stomp all over it."

"You're hung like my favorite chandelier earrings!"

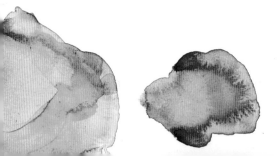

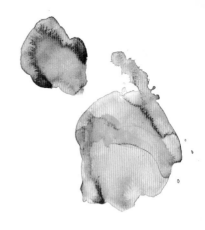

Rule 59

When it comes to fellas and footwear,
at the end of the day, comfy prevails over cute.

The importance of being comfortable in a relationship and feeling like
you can just chill can't be stressed enough. But there is such a thing as
being too cozy and worn-in (e.g., peeing with the door open), which
can have a way of making you devoid of all etiquette for the next person
you date.

Rule 60

Hudson, Tucker, Parker, and Vince are proof you can
justify love without knowing his last name.

And occasionally you're also better off not knowing how old he is or what
he does for a living.

Rule 61

Outdate yourself.

Obviously this isn't about wearing something hopelessly out of style; it's about finding a new love who surpasses the old one, or going up a size. Poor Jennifer Aniston and Stacy Keibler really had their work cut out for them. But if there's life after New York Fashion Week, surely there's life after Brad and George. Just remember this mantra: hook up, not down.

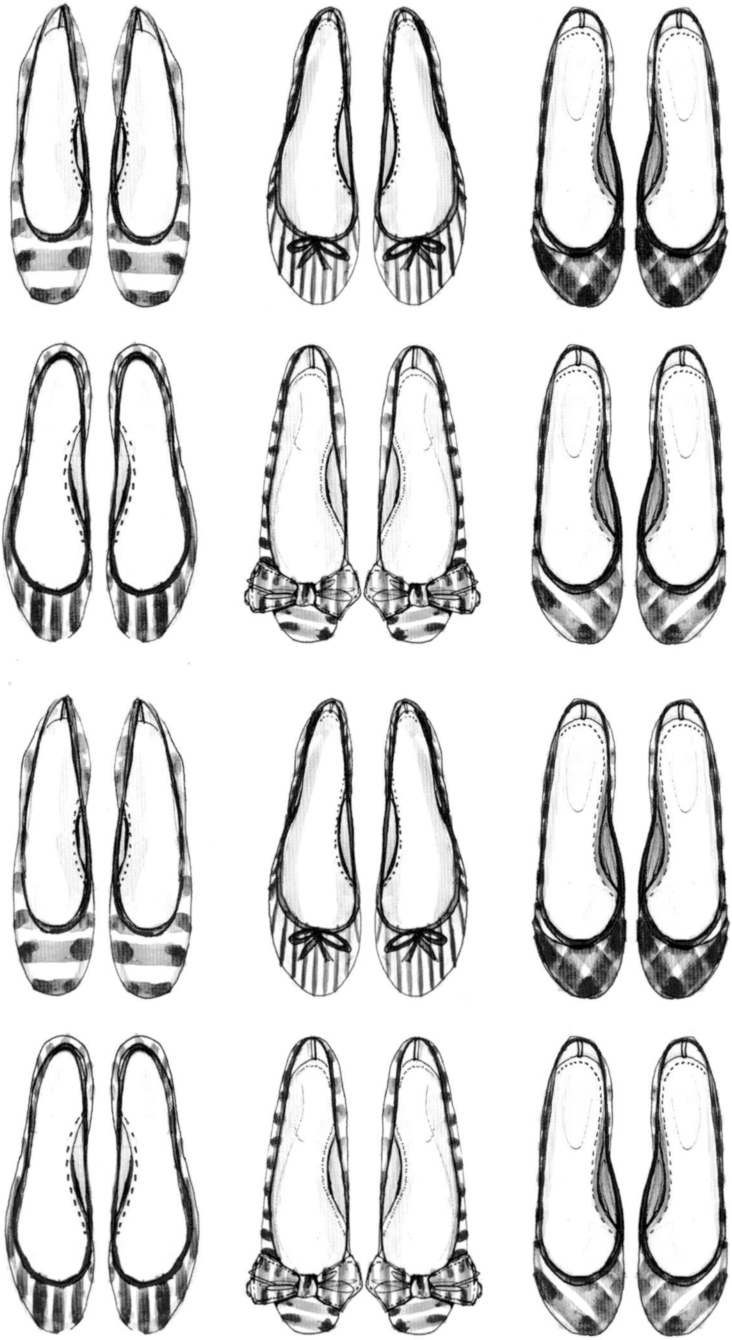

Rule 62

Buy a bigger rack? Ummm, no!

Unless it's for the shoes in your closet that desperately need organization. If a guy thinks he'd prefer you with silicone appendages and can't appreciate your huge, perky heart, make sure you have a killer outgoing message because you're never picking up your phone again. Carrie Bradshaw's machine was beeping awesome: *"I'm not home right now but my shoes are; please leave them a message."*

Rule 63

Get yourself one amazing pair of *kiss-my-boots* that put just enough swing in your backyard as you're walking away in the heat of a fight.

Check the rear view. Most shoe departments won't have a three-way mirror, so it helps to bring a compact you can hold over your shoulder. Tall styles should never add unwanted bulk to the calves or create the illusion of cankles that don't really exist. The perfect composition of sleek and sexy will make you the one he never got over. Just make sure the heels are sturdy enough that you don't wobble, hobble, or limp out of his life. You don't want him to remember you as the gimp who got away.

Rule 64

Look before you leap into any sort of final sale
arrangement for the rest of your life.

The only thing sadder than a wardrobe outgrown too quickly is a
husband who no longer fits after seventy-two days.

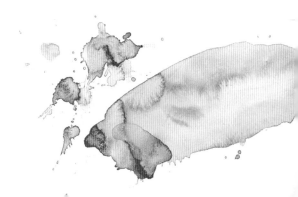

ALL VOWS FINAL.

sorry,

WE CANNOT CREDIT THE LAST
2 - 1/2 MONTHS OF YOUR LIFE
BACK. — *store management*

Rule 65

Clingy isn't a good look.

Well, technically, there's the good cling (think Blake Lively in Hervé Léger)
and then there's the needy, desperate, static kind that wants to spend every
minute of every day with you. Fall for a clinger at your own risk.

Rule 66

You need two essential messengers in your arsenal—one
who's always looking out for your best interest and one in a
rich, bold-colored leather.

When a friend is genuine enough to tell you that those pants make
you look a little heavier than you really are, or that she suspects your
boyfriend may possibly be fooling around behind your back, add her to
your A-list. Never shoot the messenger.

LIVE COLOR FULLY

Rule 67

With a little confidence you can totally pull off something daring.

Wear that red leather mini. Talk to the irresistibly attractive guy at the gym. Fate loves the fearless. P.S. Red is by far the most flirtatious of all the colors in the big book of Pantone, and it's scientifically proven to get his heart racing and stomach growling (that's right, it also triggers hunger, so use it sparingly when painting your dining room walls or surrender to a lifetime of elastic waistbands).

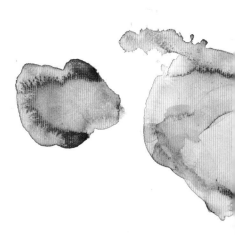

Rule 68

Malfunctions happen.

If he becomes too nervous, too drunk, or too pressured to perform in the boudoir, channel your inner performer, like Beyoncé or Janet Jackson during Super Bowl halftime and blow it off as "no biggie" (although perhaps you should be a little more sensitive about that particular phrasing). Practicing this kind of nonchalance is bound to come in handy the next time a nip-slip occurs in your favorite tube dress.

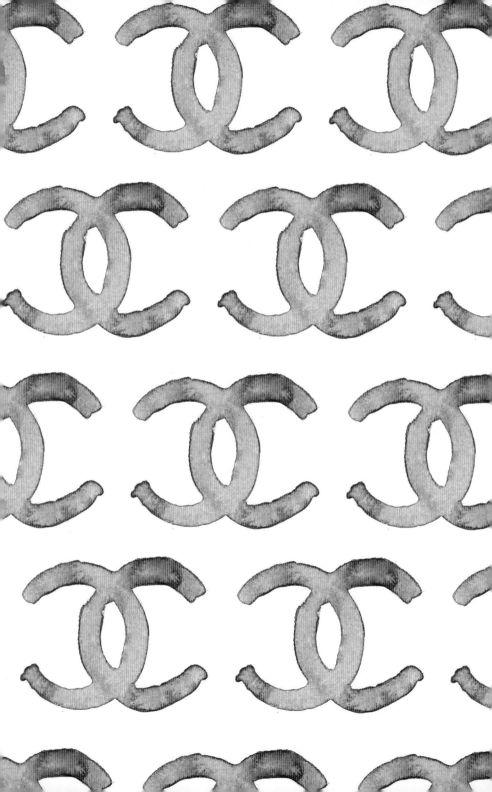

What's your shopping style?

When you're single, the whole world is a veritable department store of revolving doors and escalators leading you into the heavily fragranced unknown. So what kind of shopper are you?

The Wish Lister

You're still waiting for the perfect guy.

The Cart Abandoner

You sometimes find yourself running from something good for fear of experiencing real emotion.

The Borrower

You trust your friends' taste more than your own, occasionally pilfering their boyfriends.

The Recycler

You're notorious for dating the same exes over and over again.

The Value Huntress

You refuse to settle for anything less than what you deserve.

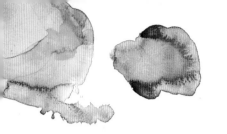

Rule 69

Wear heels in the bedroom whenever possible.

According to the cost-per-wear equation, this is the smartest way
to justify scandalously expensive shoes and mentally whittle down
your expenditure to a few dollars per day. You might as well let him
in on the fun.

*Total cost of an item ÷ estimated number of times you'll wear it = the cost per wear.

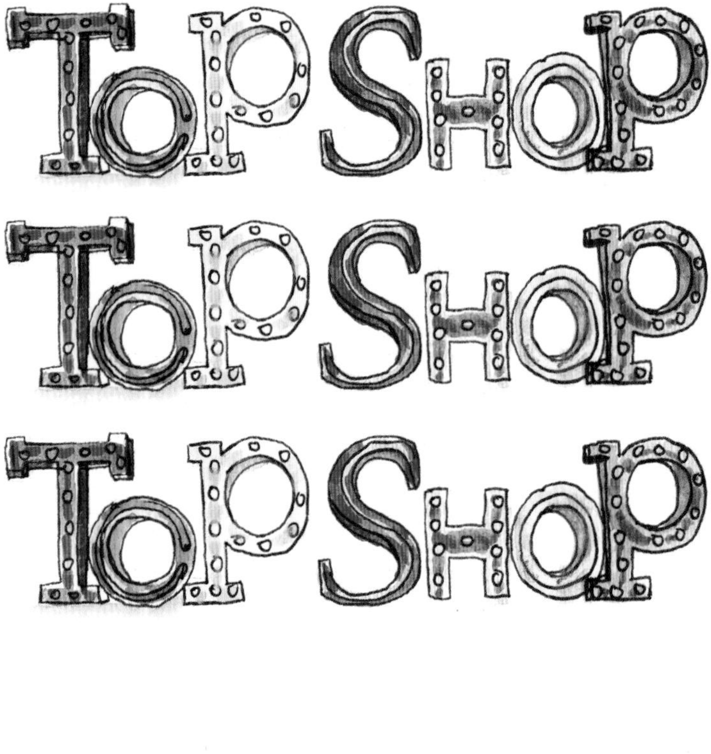
TOP SHOP
TOP SHOP
TOP SHOP

Rule 70

Make like Topshop and appoint a collaborator to boost your sales.

Always surround yourself with people who flatter you, conversationally speaking. Ideally, your wing woman won't abandon you if she meets a guy she's into, and is eager to strike up idle chatter with handsome strangers on your behalf.

Rule 71

No glove, no love.

Sage sex wisdom from the girls in the accessories department.

*Some of the hottest trends are actually accidental pregnancies. Our fave? Glittens, the totally unexpected off-spring of mittens and gloves. They're pretty much fingerless gloves with a retractable mitten for holding hands with your crush *du jour*. Brilliant.

Rule 72

Uncomfortable predicaments necessitate your most comfortable shoes. Never leave home without them.

Always keep a pair of roll-up flats in your purse in case you find yourself in a pickle of a situation and need to make a mad dash. They're a girl's best friend. Go go gadget legs!

Bar
BAR
BAR
Bar
BAR
BAR

Rule 73

Bars are the bargain basement of meeting places and should generally be avoided for this purpose.

Meeting nice men is very much like a magazine cover shoot—location is everything. Needless to say, guys trolling dive bars at closing time are probably out to get something for nothing by haggling, swindling, and low-balling you (the real danger being that bad taste suddenly starts to look sophisticated after midnight). If you do happen to meet a prospective suitor in a dimly lit bar, be sure to inspect him in the daylight before going out. The same rule goes for your foundation.

---

*This excludes denim bars, where we're pretty sure you're bound to meet a dapper gent indeed.

Dear Editrix,

I'm doing online dating for the first time and I'm about to meet my e-crush. I own a ton of flats, but what else should I pack for a proper getaway? As in getaway . . . fast . . . you know, just in case he drives a van without windows?

—Outtie 500

Dear Outtie,

The sleeker the bandage dress, the easier it is to slip out a bathroom window. If you need a sartorial "Get Out Of Jail Free" card, act like you borrowed your clothes from a friend who needs them back . . . now.

—Editrix

The "signature walk" of shame

The walk of shame (or, more accurately, the cab ride of shame) is easy to spot. Look for the girl who's inappropriately dressed in evening attire in broad daylight. If you happen to be that girl trying to make your way home with your bra in your purse, here's how to do it with dignity.

Do be resourceful. Think like a Style MacGuyver by raiding your one-night stand's bathroom cabinets. His Kiehl's moisturizer works as frizz serum, your lipstick doubles as blush, Vaseline removes eye makeup (and relieves rug burn).

Do borrow something to wear from him (especially if your outfit has sequins). Promise to return it, even if it means leaving it on his doorstep if you have no plans to see him again. If he's tall enough, you can even wear his dress shirt as a frock and cinch the waist with the whole roll of dental floss.

Do tie your hair back, even if you have to use the twisty off his bag of raisin bagels or the rubber band off the newspaper in his driveway.

Do wash off the stamp from the club that's still on your hand and marring your mani.

Do play it safe and knock designer boots at your place next time.

Rule 74

Don't be caught wearing certain things in public.

Like binoculars. In the bushes. Outside his bedroom. And never use the fashion phrase "totes obsessed" when referring to anything other than a handbag.

Rule 75

The right statement piece practically does all the work
for you when it comes to getting the attention of
broad-shouldered strangers.

An eye-catching gemstone bib necklace will get you noticed, give him
an easy opening line, and leave you with enough stories to keep you
interesting well into your nineties.

Rule 76

Go easy on the fugly florals.

Guys don't know carnations are corny. It's the thought that counts,
so always make a point to show your appreciation for the gesture.
You, on the other hand, have no excuse for dressing like an
overgrown greenhouse.

Rule 77

Men are rarely accurate about their sizes, kind of like everything at the Gap.

Did you know his definition of extra large is likely quite medium? Both men and mega retailers use arbitrary units of measurement that allow them to manipulate a woman's perception.

*This phenomenon of exaggerating numbers is officially known as vanity sizing.

Rule 78

Never wear embarrassing undergarments as insurance against dropping trou too soon.

If your willpower weakens and your date discovers them anyhow, he'll be aghast and you'll be mortified. Save yourself the trauma and leave a tornado of clothes strewn all over your place so you're less inclined to let him inside at the end of the night.

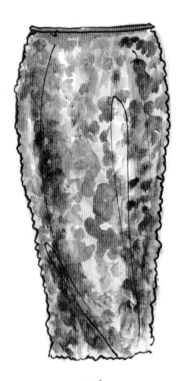

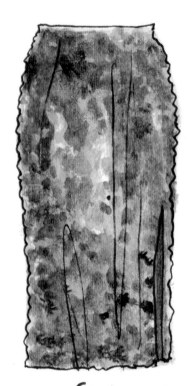

Splurge
MARC JACOBS $2,400

Steal
NASTYGAL $58

Rule 79

Embrace the highs and the lows.

A $4 H&M tank here. A $400 Botkier bag there. One night of passion. Approximately 4 days, 14 hours, and 29 minutes without hearing from him. An unpredictable high-low mix is what keeps things interesting, as any current issue of *Harper's Bazaar* will attest.

Rule 80

The "happily ever after" you read about in fairytales comes from within, just like shinier, healthier, thicker hair comes from eating at least two daily servings of iron-rich foods.

A relationship with a man will not change your relationship with yourself. Your homework? Learn to love dining alone. Take your favorite fashion magazine and a confident swagger. Don't worry, nobody's looking at you; they're too busy worrying about their own food allergies and MIA server. The best part? You don't have to share your dessert!

Strappily ever after

In Cinderella's fairytale, a winning shoe-gown combination secured her happy ending. But it seems some very important realities were left on the editing room floor. Behold the lost footage that would have shattered our collective childhood fantasies and forever changed our desire to dress up like Disney princesses for Halloween.

Belle was crestfallen when she found out Prince Adam was no beast in bed.

When Prince Charming's desire for Snow White began to wane, the magic mirror told her to lock herself in a tanning booth, bleach her hair, and double her poison (Botox).

Ariel and Prince Eric had very different interpretations of a happy ending. The wide-eyed virgin mermaid wasn't willing, so she left him turned on and writhing like a fish on dry land.

Prince Phillip suffered from depression and rarely showered. The smell of week-old horseback is what woke Sleeping Beauty. The kiss merely gave her a cold.

The Enchanted Forest was actually Prince Flynn's name for Rapunzel's thicket of hair. Down there.

*Walt Disney's leading men also appear deceivingly taller on screen. *Le sigh.*

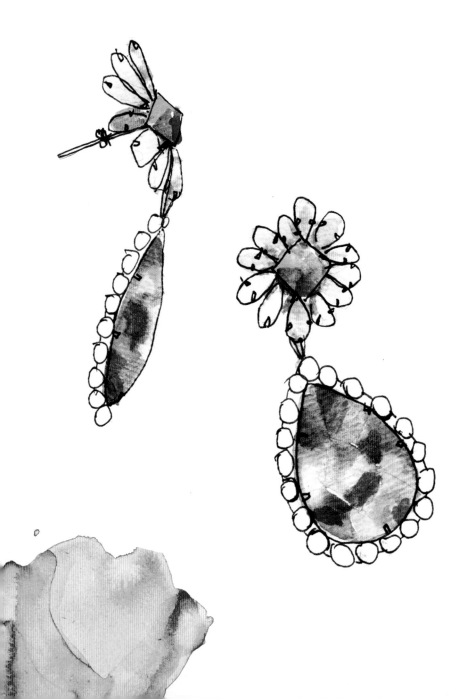

Rule 81

If you can find your jewelry and underwear in the
morning, the sex wasn't that great.

Trust us, when you can't find them, you surely won't miss them.

Rule 82

Never toil in sweat and tears trying to squeeze into the wrong relationship or the wrong shoes.

Tim Gunn's "make it work" mantra doesn't apply to romance. Dating is not like modeling, which is all about how much torture you can take (she who dies with the thickest skin wins). It's not supposed to be that hard, really.

*Did you know women who vacuum-pack themselves into skinny jeans are more likely to try to work it out with an ill-fitting boyfriend?

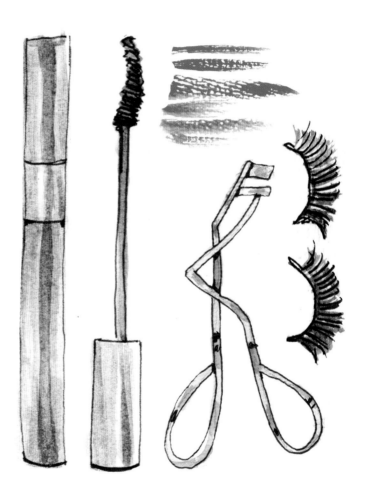

Rule 83

There are times when it's perfectly acceptable to fake it.
False lashes. Collagen injections. Go ahead, slap on some
concealer and call it sleep. But never feign any kind of
enthusiasm for things he loves that don't interest you.

The last thing you want to be is his sock puppet. Exaggerating things like
your athleticism, outdoorsy-ness, and other so-called common interests may seem like a good idea at the time, but he's bound to see right
through the act, no matter how much adidas
by Stella McCartney you own.

BAD DATE?

Redeem the rest of your night without wasting another minute.

Must be presented at the time of checkout. Cannot be combined with other excuses.

Rule 84

If your online date is nothing like advertised, you're
entitled to bounce like a bad check.

Enter code SEEYA at checkout, or use this coupon.

Closet confession

Every fall, a popular women's magazine we'll call *Kismet* publishes its annual bachelors issue, in which one stud from each state is selected from a pile of pleas submitted by sisters, mothers, and modeling agents. Olivia was flipping through the magazine on a stationary bike at the gym, looking for outfit inspiration, when she opened it to Chad, a smoldering hunk from an equally hot state, and a news reporter by profession.

She stealthily tucked the mag in her bag and ran home to send a perfume-spritzed letter to Chad's *Kismet*-sponsored PO Box. In it, she included her very best photo and introduced herself as the girl next door in a neighboring state. Just to gauge his sense of humor, she also asked if he was wearing a wig (his face was classically handsome despite the pile of hot fudge on his head).

Chad wrote back many pages, to her surprise, and was quick to clarify that his hair had been shellacked by stylists on the shoot and that he feared he'd never live it down. Just like that, they instantly bonded over hair product.

As the weeks passed, snail mail turned into rapid-fire email exchanges that were becoming longer and more detailed, and he said he looked forward to meeting her soon. Things were progressing fast, and *Sleepless in Seattle* had been on television two times that very same week, prompting Olivia to ask Chad to be her designated arm candy for an upcoming boat dance hosted by her university.

"They knew it," Annie Reed (Meg Ryan's character) had said on-screen. *"Time, distance, nothing could separate them. Because they knew. It was right. It was real."* Olivia was convinced: Chad was going to be her real-life Sam Baldwin.

Chad said *"absofrickinlutely"* to her invitation but not before asking if they could go halvsies on the cost of his airfare. *"Not to worry,"* he wrote. *"You can just mail me a check."* She hadn't anticipated the shipping fees since she would also be paying for their hotel, but gladly obliged (he later invoiced her for half of $301.23, plus the leftover penny).

The day Chad was to arrive at the airport, Olivia found herself chewing her freshly manicured fingertips, stuck in traffic on the way to pick him up. It had suddenly occurred to her that Chad could be one of those guys on *Dateline* who cons women out of money with promises of romance. Had *Kismet* magazine even bothered to do a background check? The thought was enough to send her sprinting through the terminal in towering heels.

When Olivia finally approached the United gate, it didn't immediately register that Chad was standing right in front of her. Had he not loudly quipped, *"Arm candy, at your service!"* she may have whizzed right by him.

He was admittedly buzzed on Johnny Walker and squeezed into a tight mock turtleneck, ribbed for her pleasure. Apparently he'd eaten too many peanuts on the plane, which is why he kept repeating *"food coma!"* and she couldn't help but notice he'd packed enough luggage for a one-way trip.

In person, he looked nothing like his photo, and was perhaps the only guy Olivia had ever met who loved fashion as much as her. Consequently, he spent the first hour of his arrival ironing his jeans.

Olivia was convinced she was being punished by the wrathful boat dance gods for being a tad bit superficial in her motives. What would Annie Reed do?

Fortunately, the weekend went by in a flash, except for the part where Chad wanted to fool around after the boat dance. And the part where he chipped his veneers (his hair was real, his perfect teeth were not).

While on the phone, scheduling an appointment to repair his Guy Smiley grin, Chad enunciated every word as though he were reporting a breaking news story. Olivia was kicking herself for not catching that detail earlier, but she'd never once stopped in all of her wild fantasizing and romanticizing to actually talk to Chad on the phone, which leads us to one *très* important conclusion: long distance relationships are for people who've actually met.

How to throw the pity party of the season

When things don't work out, instead of camping out in your sweats, bleating like an injured lamb, and watching movies that will bring on the waterworks, try these tips for a super *soirée*.

Do create a stellar guest list. One half should be made up of the supporters who always thought you were too good for him. The other should be made up of people you can recruit to be a part of team *moi*.

Do make it a potluck and have everyone bring a Post-It with their biggest qualm about him written on it.

Don't open less than three gift registries. Woo-hoo!

Do hire a band. A really good-looking band.

Don't do any of the cooking. Opt for fresh-baked cupcakes from the local bakery. Serve with plus-sized cocktails.

Rule 85

Beware of herpès in Hermès.

Just because he looks conservative doesn't mean he's not contagious.

Fashion plates

Takeout, make out, and home just in time to catch the eliminations on *Project Runway*? Drab date alert! Believe it or not, your extraordinary taste in clothes increases your potential for being a great cook, so find an excuse to throw a dinner party and flaunt your culinary charms. Behold a few editor-tested, boyfriend-approved recipes from the cook books stashed between our look books.

GLAM CHOPS

4 servings

4 large lamb chops
2 tablespoons butter
2 medium onions, sliced
1 medium green pepper, seeded and finely chopped
1 pound zucchini, sliced
1 pound tomatoes, skinned and sliced
Salt and freshly ground pepper to taste
1 tablespoon chopped parsley
1 teaspoon sugar

Preheat oven to 350 degrees. Melt the butter in a skillet and brown the chops quickly, then transfer them to a 2-quart casserole. Add the onions and green pepper to the skillet and sauté gently over low heat for about 10 minutes, or until soft. Cook zucchini in boiling water for 3 to 4 minutes, then drain. Add zucchini and tomatoes to onion mixture, then spoon over chops. Cover casserole and bake for 1½ hours, stirring occasionally. No additional liquid is necessary. Place the lamb chops on a warm serving dish and drain the vegetables, reserving the liquid. Spoon the drained vegetables around the meat. Garnish with parsley. Season the reserved juices to taste and add the sugar. Serve separately to spoon over lamb chops. (Source: San Francisco à la Carte)

SHRIMP LOUIS VUITTON

2 servings

1/4 cup mayonnaise
2 tablespoons purchased chili sauce
1 tablespoon Dijon mustard
1 tablespoon fresh lemon juice
1 teaspoon grated lemon peel
4 cups mixed baby greens
1 avocado, peeled, halved, pitted
10 cooked, peeled, deveined extra-large shrimp
1 green onion, finely chopped

Whisk mayonnaise, chili sauce, mustard, lemon juice, and lemon peel in small bowl to blend. Season dressing with salt and pepper. Arrange greens on 2 plates. Top greens with 1 avocado half, rounded side down. Fill avocado cavities with shrimp. Spoon dressing on top, and sprinkle with green onion. (Source: Epicurious.com)

A-LINE SKIRT STEAK
4 servings

1/2 cup olive oil
1/3 cup soy sauce
4 scallions, washed and cut in half
2 large cloves garlic
1/4 cup lime juice
1/2 teaspoon red pepper flakes
1/2 teaspoon ground cumin
3 tablespoons dark brown sugar or Mexican brown sugar
2 pounds inside skirt steak, cut into 3 equal pieces
Special tools needed: your blow dryer

Heat charcoal, preferably natural chunk, until gray ash appears. In a blender, add oil, soy sauce, scallions, garlic, lime juice, red pepper, cumin, and sugar, then puree. In a large, heavy-duty zip-top bag, put pieces of skirt steak and pour in marinade. Seal bag, removing as much air as possible. Allow steak to marinate for 1 hour in refrigerator.

Remove steak from bag and pat dry with paper towels. Using a blow dryer, blow charcoal clean of ash. Once clean of ash, lay steaks directly onto hot coals for 1 minute per side. When finished cooking, place meat in double thickness of aluminum foil, wrap, and allow to sit for 15 minutes.

Remove meat from foil, reserving foil and juices. Slice thinly across the grain of the meat. Return to foil pouch and toss with juice. Serve with grilled peppers and onions, if desired. (Source: Alton Brown, FoodNetwork)

*Slip into a floor-sweeping gown to rid the kitchen of fallen crumbs. Rain boots should also be at the ready in case of sudden dishwasher flooding.

Rule 86

Unless you're a Birkin bag, being hard to get is overrated.

Playing the aloof card can make you appear cold, bored, and disinterested—a look that only works for runway models and Victoria Posh Beckham. In fact, being easy to spot is the new hard to get, so dress accordingly.

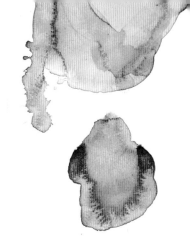

Rule 87

When it comes to fur, picket, protest, and petition for what you believe is ethically, morally, and aesthetically right.

Most guys tirelessly pluck, wax, thread, shave, and depilitate only because they think you like it.

A petition to bring sexy back

We, the undersigned, would like to revive the hairy-chested
Magnum PI look and keep manly men from going extinct.

Goal: 40 signatures, and counting . . .

Name	Signature	Address	Email
1.			
2.			
3.			
4.			
5.			
6.			
7.			
8.			
9.			
10.			
11.			
12.			
13.			
14.			
15.			
16.			
17.			

18. _____

19. _____

20. _____

21. _____

22. _____

23. _____

24. _____

25. _____

26. _____

27. _____

28. _____

29. _____

30. _____

31. _____

32. _____

33. _____

34. _____

35. _____

36. _____

37. _____

38. _____

39. _____

40. _____

Rule 88

Never doubt your intuition, the same way a celebrity who can't dress herself never doubts her stylist.

Always right: your heart and Rachel Zoe. They'll help you differentiate right from *"wrong, wrong, wrong."*

Rule 89

Every woman is born with an inner compass to help
her navigate a relationship full of lame excuses and
a clearance rack full of *lamé*.

Tap that power and chart a path to utter fabulosity.

Rule 90

Dialed him up after a few too many martinis? Blame it on one of your expensive little clutches.

Simply say, *"Oops! My handbag did the dialing, that meddling minx!"* In the event your purse really does stealthily reach out to him without consulting you first, it could mean one of two things: you should give him another chance because your handbag always knows what's best for you, or you've accidentally set up a speed dial key associated with him. Call your local service provider for details on undoing this very unfortunate setting.

Accessories to a crime

Okay Colombo, you're going to need a slim-fitting Burberry trench coat for this next exercise in supersleuthing. Aside from discovering unknown hotel bills or collecting actual DNA evidence (lipstick on his collar), there are plenty of ways to determine if your boyfriend has been engaging in foul play. The truth will always prevail, usually between his couch cushions or in his bathroom cabinets.

Consider the presence of jewelry at his place *le smoking* gun. Although an earring may innocently fall between the sofa every now and then, a ring is the type of finishing touch a woman makes great efforts to put on, and removes only when a.) going to sleep or b.) rolling up her sleeves to some kind of chore, like the dishes or a hand job.

Tread lightly with any man who has a self-proclaimed lost and found of baubles in varying tastes and styles on his nightstand. It wouldn't hurt to cast your glance upward every now and then, as necklaces and bracelets could be hanging like hunting trophies from his light fixtures (you'd have to live it to believe it).

Other incriminating items can be found in the shower. A wad of long blond hair in the drain when you're a short-haired brunette. A loofah. Perfumed shower gel. He may try to convince you that they're his mother's or sister's when they live hundreds of miles away, or that they belong to him even though he doesn't have a hairbrush or lint roller to his name.

The jig is up.

Rule 91

Getting back with your ex is like shopping at your own garage sale.

Dating your own discards again? Did you know that yo-yo dating is as unhealthy as yo-yo dieting (we think we saw that on an episode of *The Dr. Oz Show)*. We're big believers in second chances, but the third, fourth, and twelfth time is where things start to get a little dicey. Some relationships have a way of working out if you've both matured and have a newfound appreciation for one another, but usually history is bound to repeat, and just like a *Gossip Girl* rerun, you know how this storyline will end. Don't fret, you're not the only one to forget a bad idea is a bad idea: look at all the designers who bring back the unthinkable every few years only to shelve it all over again. The entire fashion industry revolves around manic regurgitation.

Rule 92

How can you be lovers if you can't be Facebook friends?

What's more obnoxious than a bad paisley print? The guy who micromanages his Facebook account just like Tiger Woods would. You see, of his 5,000 Facebook friends, 4,999 are females and potential hookups, which is why he only private messages you, untags himself immediately when you post pics of the two of you together, and deletes anything you write that may link the two of you as a couple. Keeping up appearances is a full-time job that's bound to wear him out, so it's quite possible that before you even met, he already disabled everyone from writing anything on his impenetrable wall.

Eye candy

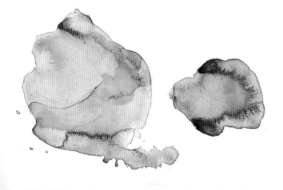

Rule 93

A purely physical attraction has about as much value as a gorgeous pair of shoes you can't walk in, or a trendy pair of sunglasses without your prescription.

Fun, yes. Functional, no.

*Always keep your prescriptions up to date so you can clearly see who you're flirting with from across the room.

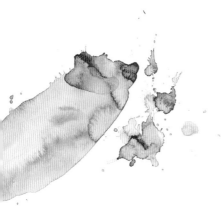

Rule 94

Single women are most vulnerable at a wedding. Never mind the open bar; the uglier the bridesmaid dress you've been forced to wear, the faster you'll want to get out of it.

Groomsmen with Taffeta Fever will always take advantage of this fact.

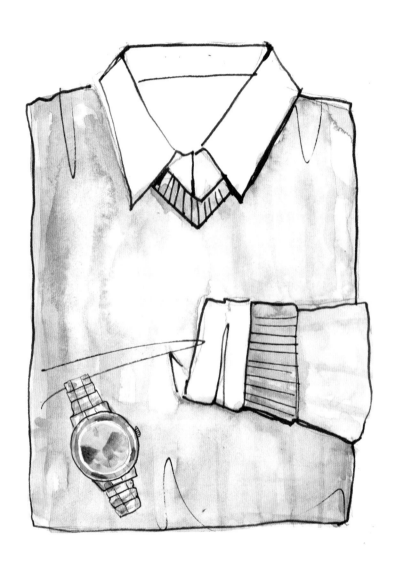

Rule 95

Just because his watch is more expensive than yours doesn't mean his time is more valuable.

"Be there in 5" could mean minutes, hours, or days depending on his perception of time and traffic. Don't let him leave you hanging like one of Helen Roper's muumuus.

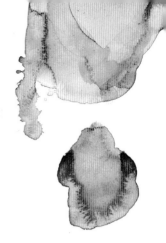

Rule 96

Ever so *Swiftly* take your breakup to the bank (hello extra shoe money).

Now's your chance to pen a multi-platinum-selling anthem about how you're *never ever ever* getting back together. Thank you, Taylor, for paving the way for such honest dating dialogue.

THE
DEVIL
WEARS

NADA

MILANO

DAL 1913

How to handle a no-makeup situation

According to the *existentialista*—the most spiritual of all the fashionistas—destiny can't be fulfilled when you're forced to dart the other way because you're not wearing makeup. Here's how to do the 5-second face when you're out of lip gloss and out of luck.

Don't shriek and run in the other direction if he's already spotted you from a distance.

Do act like nothing's wrong. Saying you're not feeling well to justify a pasty complexion or apologizing for the way you look is not an option.

Do take your hair down and tousle it over one eye like Jessica Rabbit (preferably the eye with the darkest circle or puffiest bag underneath).

Do remember that men have short memories. To erase an unfortunate image from his mind, simply make a point of running into him again when you look ravishing.

Don't leave your makeup bag home alone and start treating it like the appendage it is.

Rule 97

Never overlook a man's coordination skills.

If he coordinates brown shoes with black pants, it's almost endearing.
Not so if he doesn't coordinate your Valentine's Day plans until the last
minute when every restaurant is already booked.

Rule 98

There's plenty to adore about dating on consignment if you can get past the emotional hurdles, like the fact his ex-wife still acts like she owns him.

In the words of the fierce Tina Turner, *"What's love but a secondhand emotion?"*

Rule 99

Keep things weekend-casual.

If you're not sure how you feel about him (or can't remember what he looks like) and he wants to do dinner on Saturday night, suggest Sunday brunch with friends or a quick coffee run instead.

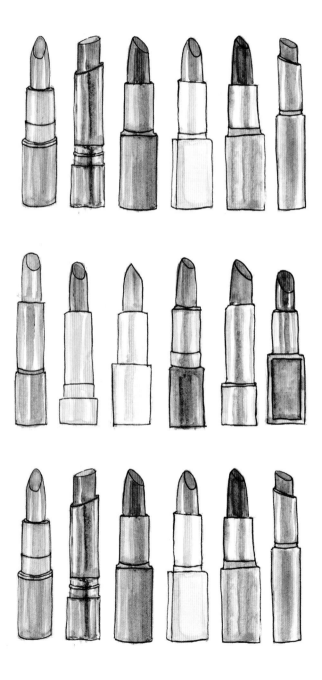

Rule 100

Being understated is overrated. Amplify every conversation with bright, notice-me lip color.

If you suspect he's not still listening, wear a louder sweater. You can confirm he's not listening by looking at his expression, which will be similar to the blank, glazed-over look you get while staring at your closet trying to pick out what to wear.

Annual dating expenses

Blowouts $200+

Spray tans $100+

Bikini waxes $300+

Hair coloring $500+

Haircuts $300+

Clothing $500+

Lingerie $100+

Shoes and Accessories $300+

*Or why you shouldn't argue all night
if he wants to pick up the tab on a
first date.

Rule 101

Sharing misplaced feelings too soon is like spilling a purse full of awkward belongings at his feet. Zip it. Zip it good.

You really don't need to tell him your heart's beating through your blouse. Follow this minimalist mantra for the first 1,500 hours or until he reveals his feelings (preferably not during sex), whichever comes first.

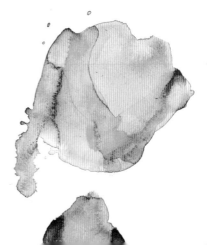

Rule 102

Muster up some selfie-esteem.

When a guy you've been dating just a short time boldly texts *"What are you wearing?"* you have three options: 1.) Show off your styling capabilities by sending him a Sartorialist-worthy shot in head-to-toe Prada, 2.) Play up your sense of humor by Googling saggy, naked old lady and texting your findings to him, 3.) If nude is your best color, unleash the Victoria's Secret model within and strike a scantily clad pose, but not before experimenting with your best angle, finding your most flattering backlighting, and cropping out your face. Have you learned nothing from Scarlett Johansson's nude foible photos?

selfie (noun) A self-portrait photograph that, when taken without clothes, has been known to cause chronic *reply-arrhea*

Rule 103

Chains won't hold a relationship together.

But a quilted chain cross-body bag embossed with Chanel's Double Cs
will show the unpaid interns whose boss.

Rule 104

To catch a guy's gaze across a crowded room, smile with your eyes like Tyra.

Miss Banks currently has 275 silent-but-deadly smiles in her arsenal, including the "angry but still smiling" smile, which is sure to come in handy when you catch him ogling other women. She famously calls this *smizing*, but *smeaving*—or smiling with your cleavage—can be useful too. Fair-skinned maidens can get the look by brushing a bit of bronzer between the breasts. Tan or deliciously chocolate complexions can use a shimmering champagne highlighter to create the illusion of Grand Canyon depth. *Viola!* A beaming bustline.

Dating tips & tricks from the beauty department

Prevent frown lines by not holding in important conversations.

Don't let anyone with bad eyebrows set you up on a blind date.

Never go to sleep without washing off your makeup or resolving an argument.

Master two looks in the event he's now dating someone much younger than you: the smoky eye and the stink eye, both of which command the right kind of attention across a crowded room.

Questions to ponder: Do you see him less frequently than you see your hairdresser for trims? Does he flee after sex at the speed of a quick-dry topcoat? Is he jealous of everyone, including your vibrating mascara wand?

Always carry travel-size extra-hold hairspray. It's cheaper than pepper spray but just as effective.

Honesty is the best policy, starting with your bathroom lighting.

Mr. Right is as elusive as a great hairstylist. Seek referrals from trusted friends.

Don't date a guy if he has bangs or uses that word as a verb.

Love your beauty sleep? Don't marry an incurable morning person. Chronic 5 a.m. wakeup calls are murder on the under eyes and a general lack of sleep is believed to make you gain weight faster than a bucket of deep-fried Cheetos.

Rule 105

Like Lady Gaga in a meat dress at an awards show, a guy may try to pull off something utterly ridiculous just to see what he can get away with.

He may say *"Why didn't you call me?"* when he said he'd call you or *"Why didn't you show up?"* when he didn't tell you where to go.

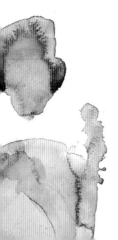

Rule 106

Take the stress out of first date dressing by treating it like a fashion shoot.

What you'll need: multiple changes of wardrobe, a killer playlist, and a girlfriend to play the role of André Leon Tally, trusted *dreckitude* advisor. A foldable rail will help you compile your edit and a steamer will make hard-to-iron fabrics appear crisp and polished. As you're putting together your outfit, play a little game we call *Frock-Paper-Scissors*. Dresses beat pants. Heels beat flats. Color beats black. We always advise erring on the overdressed side, as it simply implies you were expecting to go somewhere a little more festive and that you have the confidence to dress up for yourself and nobody else. Showing up underdressed is as if to say, *"I haven't a thing to wear!"*

Rule 107

Someday your prints will come.

Patiently waiting can be the hardest part. Just ask anyone who's purchased anything from Net-A-Porter and opted for the 4–6 day standard ground shipping.

Rule 108

Channel the willpower of a window shopper and look-but-
don't-touch for at least three weeks postbreakup.

That's not to say you can't start lining up dates, but give yourself some
time to heal and stop fantasizing about running into your ex while
looking cozy with your new guy.

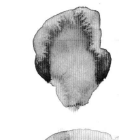
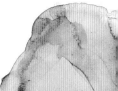

Rule 109

Don't let him talk you into having his initials
monogrammed on your body like a Louis Vuitton bag.

Opt for his-and-hers towels, not tattoos.

Rule 110

Timing is everything when it comes to drop-crotch harem pants and marriage proposals.

Gracefully accept the fact that the world may not be ready for the return of what appear to be MC Hammer pants, and that your boyfriend may not be ready to get married when you are. Being too ahead of your time is a curse only the truly fashion-forward understand. Wear the new shredded denim trend too soon and people on the street will think you're a derelict. Meet a man prematurely and you won't become his wife; you'll become his dress rehearsal—the one teaching him how to stop snoring, make *crème brûlée*, and apologize convincingly—all to be enjoyed by the next woman who comes along.

Rule 111

A man should never sound like a Nike commercial
in the bedroom.

"C'mon, just do it."

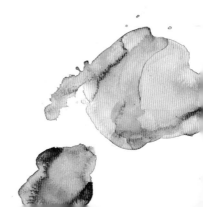

Rule 112

To truly appreciate a gem, you may need to look at him in a different light.

One day you begin to notice his rare brilliance, his dazzling sense of humor, and holy Hanes are his abs cut! It's like Cupid has been asleep at the wheel for the last six years. Honestly, the best relationship grows out of friendship, slowly but surely, at the pace of botched bangs.

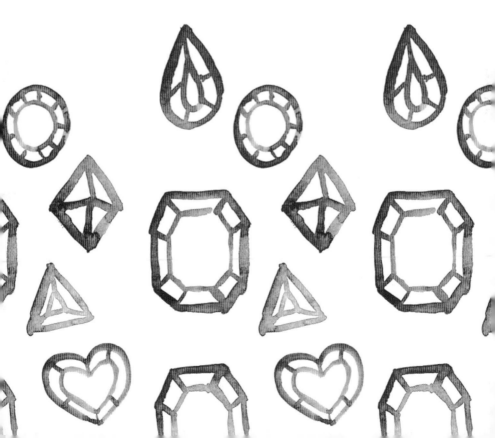

Rule 113

Surely you love big fancy bows on your shoes and in your hair, but just because he slapped one on a box of Turbotax software with the rebate already cut out of the box doesn't make it a birthday gift.

Pity the fool who gives you a gift card, a rain check, or something he cleared out of his desk drawer. You may want to take careful precautions to avoid giving his sister compliments on her hideous purse during a moment of awkward silence or you may get the exact same one. *Surprise!*

Rule 114

After a breakup, invest in a pair of Oliver Peoples glasses
with rose-colored lenses to keep yourself wildly optimistic.

Your future's so bright, you're going to need them. Did we mention
there's no better way to hide a love-scorned hangover?

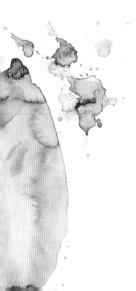

Plus-size cocktails

Don your drinking caps, dolls! It turns out there's a cocktail for every kind of cruel and unusual breakup. And guess what? Playing with booze is like dressing for your body type—it's all about proportion (and, in this case, the heavier, the better).

THE DIRTY HOUDINI-TINI
6+ oz vodka

1 dash dry vermouth

1 oz brine from olive jar

In a mixing glass, combine vodka, dry vermouth, brine, and olives. Consider adding quantity to ingredient list. Pour into a glass over ice and drink on the rocks, or strain into a chilled cocktail glass.

THE CHEATA-RITA
2+ oz tequila made from 100 percent agave,
reposado, or blanco

1 oz Cointreau

1 oz freshly squeezed lime juice

Salt or edible glitter for garnish

Combine tequila, Cointreau, and lime juice in a cocktail shaker filled with ice. Moisten the rim of your margarita glass with water and dip it into the salt or glitter. Shake, strain, pour, and serve.

THE "IT'S NOT YOU, IT'S ME" MAI TAI
2+ oz aged rum

3/4 oz freshly squeezed lime juice

1/2 oz orange curaçao

1/4 oz rich simple syrup, also known as rock
candy syrup

1/4 oz orgeat syrup

1 cup crushed ice

1 mint sprig, for garnish

Combine all ingredients in a cocktail shaker, shake vigorously, and pour the entire contents into a double Old Fashioned glass. Garnish with the mint sprig.

Rule 115

Beware of invitations that are breezier than a sundress.

Someday is not a day of the week.

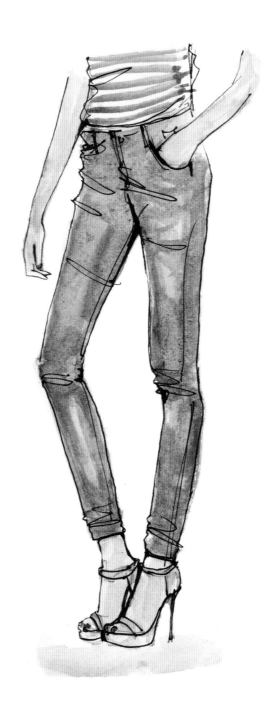

How to peg a bad boy like a pair of jeans

Bad boys are like breakouts. Your goal is to fend them off before they erupt into something full-fledged.

Does he own a leather moto jacket that smells distinctly of asphalt and women's perfume?

Does he cause you heartbreak, then pin you against a wall to kiss and make up?

Does he outwardly own his badness and say things like *"I don't deserve you."*

Does he call or text only while drinking, or after 11 p.m.?

Does he get all twitchy when you touch his unlocked phone?

Does he leave his underwear behind on your floor and never even realize they're gone?

Does he always call you *babe* instead of using your real name?

babe (noun) 1. What a guy calls you when he's forgotten your name. 2. Rachel Zoe's pet name for her husband, Roger, as uttered by her every 10–15 seconds on The Rachel Zoe Project. (*"Babe, don't just sit there watching Fashion Police, come and help me deal with this real-life fashion disaster happening in our living room right now, babe. Babe? Babe!"*)

*This message is brought to you by HPV (an association of Heartbreak Prevention Volunteers).

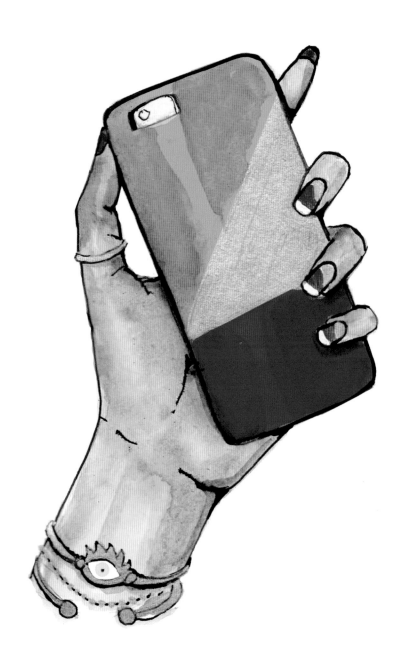

Rule 116

Text messages are the sweatpants of interpersonal communication. *Lazy!*

Texts serve as gentle reminders of all the things men should do but don't. Namely, ironing their shirts, engaging in foreplay, and calling to ask you out. Texting is really meant to be succinct, and a supplement to other communication. If he repeatedly asks you out this way and it's wreaking havoc on your monthly data allowance or causing grave misunderstandings, respond with something flirty like, *"I miss your voice."* If he doesn't take the hint, tell him you dislike texts, or that you lost your phone somewhere over the Atlantic Ocean and see if he makes an effort to call you at home.

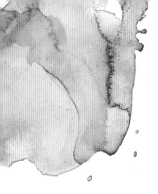

Rule 117

It's hard to have a healthy relationship with anyone who's obnoxiously faded like acid-wash jeans.

For one thing, it's really important to be having the same conversation at the same time. When he's stoned, he may not remember certain things. A lot of certain things. Please don't let him resort to comparing his Mary Jane addiction to yours. We assure you the shoes are a lot more productive than the drugs.

Rule 118

Marry fresh out of high school and develop a terrible itch akin to a bad poly blend.

High school is a very confusing and hormone-ridden place. There are so many things that seemed really cool back then, like Scott Baio, tiny dresses with t-shirts underneath, and your boyfriend who loved ditching Spanish class with you in the trunk of his car. If you marry the first and only guy you've ever dated, down the road you'll inevitably wonder what you missed out on.

Rule 119

Don't push a man down the aisle, whether it's the aisle at the little white church or the aisle where they keep the nail polish at the beauty supply store.

You know how you feel about Home Depot? Well, that's how he feels about Sephora. To guys, it's just a lot of boring spackle and paint. A majority of them admit they loathe shopping missions, especially the ones where they have to sit in a chair as you try on jeans. He may make the experience as miserable as possible so you'll never invite him along again. If he's not there to help, he's in the way.

Dear John, I'm Gone. No More Love. (Sorry.)

How to write a lipstick letter like you mean it

Compose your masterpiece in fire engine red. Pink is too sugary-sweet, coral is too indecisive (somewhere in between the two), and nudes don't have nearly the impact or staying power.

Lengthier prose is easier transcribed in long-wearing lip liner.

A lip brush will give you better control. If finger painting is more your style, try a pot of rouge.

Set your masterpiece with a dusting of loose powder.

Don't gloss the truth.

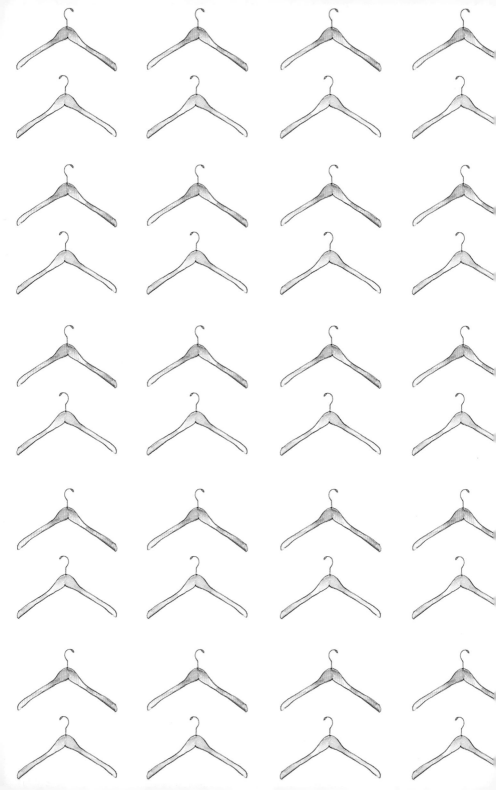

Rule 120

When it comes to relationships and closets, some of us
need more space.

Feel free to quote us on that.

Rule 121

Learn from New York Fashion Week and don't let undesirables into your—ahem—VIP area without the requisite paperwork and identity check.

Every now and then, a guy may pretend to be someone he's not just to sneak past the velvet ropes of your life. You've got to increase your security and make sure he's not hogging a prime seat for your real knight in shining Armani. This is precisely why we created the standard Curate-A-Date application, so you can curate your suitors the way you curate your wardrobe.

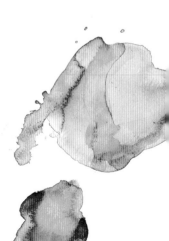

Curate-a-Date

Thank you for your interest in dating me. Due to the high volume of interested applicants, I will not be able to reply to all. However, I will respond within 8–10 weeks if you are still in the running to become *America's Next Top Boyfriend*. No follow-up phone calls, please.

Alias(es) _____

Nickname(s) _____

Twitter handle _____

Remind me where we met _____

Full name _____

Hometown _____

Date of birth _____

Hair color _____

Eye color _____

Vision left eye _____

Vision right eye _____

Height _____

Weight _____

Shoe size _____

Measurements for future gifts _____

Occupation _____

Education _____

IQ _____

Credit score _____

Best number to reach you _____

Rank the following on a scale of 1 to 10 (1 being your worst trait and 10 being your best):

Kindness _____
Patience _____
Punctuality _____
Conversation _____
Sense of humor _____
Manners _____
Helpfulness _____
Generosity _____
Personal hygiene _____
Personal style _____
Sexual prowess _____

List celebrity look-alikes:

_____
_____

List celebrity crushes:

_____
_____

List hobbies, interests, and extracurricular activities:

_____
_____

Have you ever dated any of my friends, family members, or co-workers? List their names here:

_____
_____

Do you have a reputation in the area that I should be aware of? Please specify:

_____
_____

Describe your perfect first date:

_____

_____

List your most recent ex's name and phone number in the space allotted and state the specific reason(s) for your breakup:

_____

_____

Complete this sentence: I would do anything for love except _____.

Are you currently active on an online dating site? Y/N

Have you ever been convicted of a felony? Y/N

Has a restraining order ever been filed against you? Y/N

Do you have any mental or sexual dysfunctions that cannot be treated by a doctor? Y/N

Are you currently taking any medications or performance-enhancing drugs? Y/N
List here: _____

When was the last time you had sex?
_____ a few hours ago _____ a few days ago _____ a few months ago
_____ a few years ago _____ still waiting for the right girl

Do you partake of drugs? Y/N
List here: _____

If so, is there a possibility of memory loss, brain damage, or reproductive harm? Y/N

Do you have piercings/tattoos/body hair? Please specify where:

_____

Do you get along with your parents? Y/N

Can you pretend to get along with my parents? Y/N

Do you want children? Y/N

Are you capable of remodeling a closet? Y/N

Are you against dressing up animals in clothing? Y/N

What time do you wake up on weekends?

_____

Approximately how much bathroom counter space and time do you require to get ready in the morning?

_____

How often do you travel for work?

_____

Do you have any allergies I should know about (e.g., dogs, cats, Monogolian faux fur)?

_____

Check applicable sleep conditions:
_____ sleep apnea _____ snoring _____ bed-wetting _____ sleepwalking
_____ sleep-talking _____ random thrashing _____ cover-hogging
_____ excessive drooling _____ caffeine addiction _____ must wear retainer

Hypothetical situation: we're at a casino and you win big with the quarter I gave you. Who gets the money?
A.) You (the applicant)
B.) Me (the one who loaned you the money)
C.) We split the winnings
D.) Other: _____

And, lastly, a 2-part essay question. Would *you* date *you*? Why or why not?

_____
_____
_____
_____
_____
_____
_____
_____
_____
_____
_____
_____
_____
_____
_____
_____
_____
_____
_____

Trace an outline of your hand on the back of this form and spray it with the cologne you wear. Attach one baby picture, three references, and a copy of your current immunization records.

I ATTEST THAT THESE ANSWERS ARE TRUE AND CORRECT TO THE BEST OF MY KNOWLEDGE UNDER PENALTY OF PERJURY.

X _____ Signature of applicant

X _____ Signature of witness

*A $10 processing fee may be imposed for applications that fail the requisite background, credit, and mental health checks.

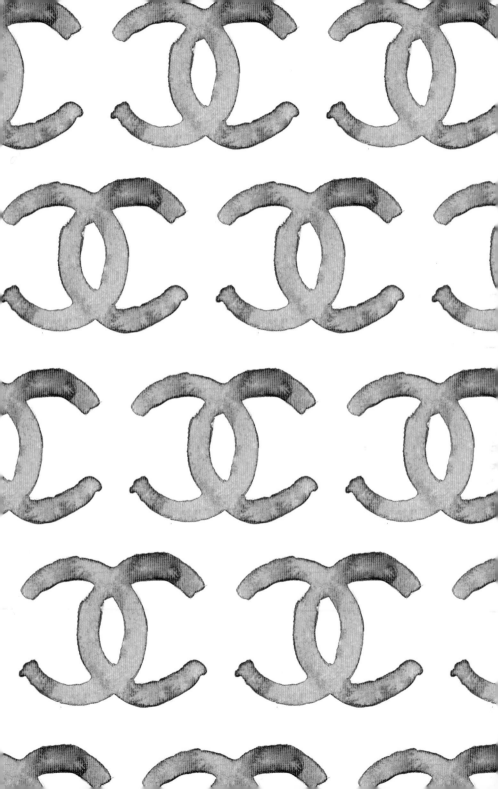

Little Black Book

A place to jot down the names and
numbers of the men you adore.

Name	Number
Michael Kors	212-452-4685
Jimmy Choo	212-759-7078
Giuseppe Zanotti	212-650-0455
Marc Jacobs	212-343-1490
Oscar De La Renta	212-288-5810
Manolo Blahnik	212-582-3007
Christian Louboutin	212-396-1884
Christian Dior	212-466-2802
Emilio Pucci	212-752-4777
Giorgio Armani	212-988-9191

About the creators

Stephanie Simons (left) is a San Francisco–born editorial strategist and television beauty expert whose work has appeared in countless regional and national publications including *DailyCandy*, *InStyle*, and *US Weekly*. She specializes in product naming and advertising campaigns for global retail brands, and credits her Grandma Fifi for her love affair with little illustrated books and the perfect coral lipstick.

Malia Carter (right) is the creator of DeepFriedFreckles.com, a popular illustration blog featuring fashion and celebrities, and named after her favorite accessories: her freckles. Her watercolor illustrations have been featured by *Teen Vogue*, Kingsrowe Gallery, and numerous fashion blogs worldwide. She lives in Columbus, Ohio, where she carries her paintbrushes with her everywhere she goes.